# Experiencing the Depths of God the Father:

## A Deeper Understanding of the Godhead

By

**Prophetess Mary J. Ogenaarekhua**

# Endorsements

"*Experiencing the Depths of God the Father* by Prophetess Mary Ogenaarekhua, a.k.a., Mary O. is a testimony that God Himself wants us to know Him and to experience Him in a greater measure. God said in **Amos 3:7** that <u>He reveals His secrets unto His servants the prophets</u>. Therefore, you will find glorious secrets about this Almighty and All-Knowing Majesty on High that loves His children without limits as He reveals Himself in an awesome journey through the chapters of this book. I encourage you to read this book because, '<u>It is the glory of God to conceal a thing: but the honor of kings is to search out a matter</u> -**Proverbs 25:2**.'"


**–Lynne Garbinsky, Chief Operations Officer, THGP/MJM, Atlanta, Georgia.**

# Dedication

I dedicate this book to God the Father. LORD God, You gave me the words to write in this book and I thank You for it because without Your teaching, I will not have anything to write. I also thank You for giving me the grace to write what You taught me. You have done through me concerning this book as it is written in **Psalm 68:11**:

> *"The Lord gave the word: great was the company of those that published it."*

Thanks Father for teaching me about Yourself, about Your Son and about Your Holy Spirit. It is a great honor to have You as my Father and my Teacher. May this book bring You much glory in Jesus name.

I also dedicate this book to all those who seek to know God on a deeper level. Never forget that God and His Word are ONE.

# Experiencing the Depths of God the Father:
## A Deeper Understanding of the Godhead

Unless otherwise indicated, all scriptures are quoted
from the King James Version of the Bible.

Published by: **To His Glory Publishing Company, Inc.**
463 Dogwood Drive, NW
Lilburn, GA  30047
(770) 458-7947
www.tohisglorypublishing.com

**This Book is available at:**
Amazon.com, BarnesandNoble.com, Booksamillion.com,
UK, Canada, Australia, etc.

Also, see the **Order Form** at the back of this book or
call/email below to order this book.

Email: tohisglorypublishing@yahoo.com
**(770) 458-7947**
**www.tohisglorypublishing.com**

**ISBN:** 978-0-9821900 -7- 4  or   0-9821900-7-7

# Table of Contents

## Chapter 5:
## Knowing God by Names that Reveal
## His Functions ...........................................95

## Chapter 6:
## Understanding the Wrath and the Fierce
## Side of God .............................................137

## Chapter 7:
## Understanding the Meaning of the Word GOD.......159

Chapter 8:
**God's Blank Check to Every Human Being** .......169

# Preface

This book is the first in a series of three books titled, *Experiencing the Depths of God the Father, Experiencing the Depths of Jesus Christ,* and *Experiencing the Depths of the Holy Spirit.* I wrote them to help people gain a deeper knowledge of God the Father, God the Son and God the Holy Spirit.

My belief is that if you are going to be totally devoted or sold out to follow God, then you owe it to yourself to know Him in depth and to understand the mysteries that He has coded in His Word to help you understand Him as you walk with Him. Therefore, it is my desire that after you have read this book, you will know God in a much deeper and intimate way than most people can ever dream of.

Remember that what made the difference between the man Moses and the rest of the children of Israel was the fact that <u>Moses knew God and he knew God's ways while the children of Israel only knew the acts of God</u>:

> **"He made known <u>his ways</u> unto Moses, <u>his acts</u> unto the children of Israel"** (Psalm 103:7).

It is His desire that you know Him intimately. I encourage you therefore to begin your journey of getting to know God in a deeper way now. May He bless you as you read this book.

**—Prophetess Mary J. Ogenaarekhua**

# Acknowledgements

I thank God Almighty for inspiring me to write this book about Him, and the other two books in this series about His Son and His Holy Spirit. Thanks Father for calling me to rise up and to write what You desire for Your people to know about You in these last days.

Thank You for the call for me to rise up as a scribe in Your house and to write what You taught me about the Godhead. To You be all the glory in the name of the Lord Jesus. Amen.

I also like to thank my fellow Christians whose hunger for a deeper knowledge of the Godhead created the opportunity that the Lord used to stir me up to arise and put in a written form for them what He has taught me about Himself. Thank you all for your intense hunger for more knowledge of God and His kingdom. May He bless you all and all those who will read this book with a greater understanding of Himself.

.

# Chapter 1
# The Origin of God

## Definition of God

**By God we mean the Supernatural Creator or the one who made the heavens and the earth. The Being** that is perfect in power, wisdom, and goodness. We worship Him as **Lord, Savior, Protector, Ruler** of the universe, etc. We know that He is **Omniscience** (has infinite knowledge), **Omnipotence** (has unlimited power), **Omnipresence** (present everywhere), **Omnibenevolence** (has perfect goodness), and that He is **eternal**.

He is the Righteous Judge; His ways are just, He cannot lie and He does not fail. He is operating His kingdom here on earth with His Son Jesus Christ through His Church; the believers. He does not change and He will not change His kingdom rules for anyone.

He defends the oppressed, the widowed and the orphaned. He is "the man of war" and He can pour out His love, His anger and His mercy abundantly. He wants all humanity to worship Him alone and to fear Him. Therefore, it is in our best interest to know Him.

**This book is not a study in apologetics or a thesis on the existence of God because we who came to Him through His Son Jesus Christ, truly believe in His existence. We are already fully persuaded that He exists and we are the living proof of it. As His children that are born of His Holy Spirit, we carry His Holy Spirit inside of us as a constant witness that He exists.** We also have further proof in the Word of God and through our daily interactions with Him that He exists and that He is the source of all existence.

<u>To set the record straight about who the real God is, when we say **God** in Christendom,</u> **we mean the God of Abraham,**

**the God of Isaac and the God of Jacob.** This distinction is critical because there are so many entities referred to as "god" today that are not the Judeo-Christian God of the Bible. We do not acknowledge them as God; neither do we support any belief in them. Therefore this book is strictly about the Judeo-Christian God of the Bible; the only Living and the only True GOD.

## Different Levels of Our Knowledge of God

Each one of us that is a Christian know God on our own personal or individual level but if you were to take a look from God's perspective at the different levels at which we all know Him, you will be surprised at how a lot of Christians only have **a very shallow or an elementary knowledge** of Him. They have no intimate knowledge of Him nor do they have daily fellowship with Him. There are a lot of believers that have never personally interacted with Him. This is sad because He so wants to interact with them on a daily basis.

**What I am saying is that a lot of Christians have not pressed into God to receive the secrets or the mysteries about Him that He reserves for those who will take the time to diligently seek to know Him deeper.** There are several levels on which you can know God and the general level is the most elementary level of the knowledge of God. His desire is that we all have a deep and well grounded knowledge of Him because **the level at which you know Him will determine how far you can go with Him concerning the things that He has prepared for you to receive here on earth.**

Getting to know Him intimately with His spoken and written Word separates the "babes" from those who are "mature" in the knowledge of Him. It is what makes the difference between those who claim to know God and those who truly know Him. You can excel in your gifts and talents from God without growing or developing an intimate knowledge of Him. **This is why Jesus boldly declared to us** in Matthew 7:21-23 that on the last day, there will be people who performed miracles, signs and wonders in His name but did not take the time to know Him:

> "Not everyone that saith unto me, Lord, Lord, shall enter into the kingdom of heaven; but he that doeth the will of my Father which is in heaven. 22 <u>Many will say to me in that day, Lord, Lord, have we not prophesied in thy name? and in thy name have cast out devils? and in thy name done many wonderful works?</u> 23 And then will I profess unto them, I never knew you: depart from me, ye that work iniquity."

One of the reasons that He is going to reject such people is because knowing God is more important to God than us doing things for Him or just knowing His acts. I say to you therefore, that **it is possible to be preaching, teaching and working miracles with your God-given gifts and grace without knowing God intimately because according to Romans 11:29, the gifts and the calling of God are without repentance:**

> "...For the gifts and calling of God **are without repentance.**"

God does not withdraw His gifts from a person; rather He will demand that the person give Him an account of how the person used the gifts in his or her lifetime. Therefore, no one will be able to claim that they did not have enough time to operate the gifts according to God's will because a lifetime is plenty of time to get something right.

Knowing God intimately is something that we have all been called to do because **He created us to know Him and to have fellowship with Him.** The difference between the God of the Bible and Buda, Krishna, Allah and all the other gods is

17

that our God lives, responds to petitions, talks to His children, visits His children and enjoys intimate fellowship with His children. This is something that all the other entities that people refer to as god or gods cannot do for their followers because they are not alive and they have no power whatsoever to save, to help, to heal or to do anything else.

**This is also one of the reasons why Christians do not run amok all over the world in riots burning up things and killing people who speak against our God or burn the Holy Bible in our attempts to protect and defend our God. We do not do these things because our God is a LIVING GOD and He sees and hears all things so He is well able to defend Himself!** My belief is that any deity or entity set up by man as "god" that cannot defend itself but has to depend on its followers to defend it, is not a "God" to be worshipped by anyone. Again, we are fully persuaded about the might, the ability and the power of our God to arise and deal with His enemies by Himself. He will also arise on our behalf and defend us when we call on Him to do so. He does not need for us to defend Him through lawless acts because He defends Himself and He defends us.

## The Beginning of God or the "Dateless Past"

According to **Psalm 90:1-2,** God has always existed from the **"dateless past"** and the Bible refers to this as **"the beginning"** in the book of **Genesis** or as far as man can actually remember. He has always been God in the entire scheme of things; before He formed the heavens and before He made the earth:

> **"Lord, thou hast been our dwelling place in all generations. 2 <u>Before the mountains were brought forth, or ever thou hadst formed the earth and the world, even from everlasting to everlasting, thou art God.</u>"**

**God has always been from everlasting or the beginning and what is revealed to us from the book of Genesis onward is really a documentation of His dealing with man since He created Adam.** Day one *(earthly time)* of His dealings with man began when He restored the earth and before He created Adam as recorded in **Genesis 1:1-28:**

> "**In the beginning God** created the heaven and the earth. 2 And the earth was without form, and void; and darkness was upon the face of the deep. And the Spirit of God moved upon the face of the waters. 3 And God said, Let there be light: and there was light. 4 And God saw the light, that it was good: and God divided the light from the darkness. 5 And **God called the light Day**, and **the darkness he called Night** *(the beginning of our earthly time)*…
>
> 26 And God said, Let us make man in our image, after our likeness: and **let them have dominion** <u>over the fish of the sea, and over the fowl of the air</u>, and <u>over the cattle</u>, **and over all the earth**, and **over every creeping thing that creepeth upon the earth**. 27 So God created man in his own image, in the image of God created he him; **male and female created he them**.
>
> 28 And God blessed them, and God said unto them, **Be fruitful**, and **multiply**, and **replenish the earth**, and **subdue it**: and **have dominion** <u>over the fish of the sea</u>, and <u>over the fowl of the air</u>, **and over every living thing that moveth upon the earth**."

Although God existed in eternity and from eternity, it was from the time that He created Adam that the history of God in our lives as we know it began. When we get to heaven, we are going to know all the things that we desire or that we are supposed to know concerning the universe before Adam was created but the account given in the Bible is the account of God's dealing with the man He created and the earth that He gave to the man to rule over.

**The thing that we need to remember is that man is not the first of God's created being to inhabit the earth.** The entities that we refer to as demons, evil spirits or devils today were once the **beings** that inhabited the earth and Lucifer (now satan or the devil) was given charge over them by God because they constituted the sanctuaries or the congregations that were on earth at that time. Adam was created as a replacement of these beings and of Lucifer because of their rebellion against God.

In Chapter 2 of my book titled "**How to Discern and Expel Evil Spirits,**" I wrote in detail about this and about who the demons that we are wrestling with today are. In the same chapter, I showed from scriptures that they were the beings or entities that first inhabited this earth and that they were judged during the fall of Lucifer. As a result of their sin in taking sides with Lucifer, God's judgment that came upon them was to strip them of their terrestrial bodies; bodies that had allowed them to move about on earth just the way man moves about on earth today.

Until the Lord reveals this to you when you read the book of Ezekiel, you are not going to know about the things that happened on earth before Adam was created. Not every Christian has a desire to know this so God in His wisdom has hidden it in His Word and He only reveals it to those who know Him and who want to know how He operates. According to **Psalm 25:14**, God will reveal His secrets to those who walk in reverential fear of Him and who obey His Word. To fear the Lord means to obey His Word:

> "**The secret of the LORD** is with them that **fear him**; and he will shew them his covenant (*secrets*)."

**What we want to know is; who is this God that we are following?** One of the reasons we need to know this is because, **if you do not know Him in the way that He wants you to know Him, you run the risk of following Him in your own way and according to your own rules and at the end, He will tell you that He never knew you.** In other words, you run the risk of Him telling you; "wait a minute, you and I never really transacted business: you thought you were following me but you were really doing your own thing which is nothing but iniquity as far as I am concerned. You used your free will to live for yourself."

## There is Only One God

God wants us to know that He alone is God and that there is none else. Therefore, He tells us things about Himself in His own words in Isaiah 45 that will help us to know and understand Him. **In the Scripture below, you will see that God is addressing not just the children of Israel but all of humanity all over the world as He tells us about Himself. He wants all humanity to know that there is only ONE GOD and that He is the one speaking to us in Isaiah 45:5-7:**

> "I am the LORD, and there is none else, there is no God beside me: I girded thee, though thou hast not known me: 6 **That they may know from the rising of the sun, and from the west, that there is none beside me. I am the LORD, and there is none else.** 7 I form the light, and create darkness: I make peace, and create evil: I **the LORD do all these things...**"

As you can see above, He declared that He is the one that formed the light and created darkness and that He made peace as well as evil. He alone can take responsibility for creating man, the earth and all that you see in it as well as the heaven and all that is in it. God takes responsibility for His creation and He is more than willing to defend His work and to personally teach anyone who desires to learn about His creation. God is Almighty and His Words are spirit and they are life; His Words have power. When God speaks a Word, the Word goes forth like a missile and it locks into its target and it powerfully performs whatever God sent it to perform. It cannot fail nor return with its mission unaccomplished!

God also declared that He created evil. <u>This does not mean that He created sin but He will recompense an evil person with their own evil deeds or wickedness because He is the "Defender of the Oppressed" and the "Recompenser of the wicked."</u> Meaning that He recompenses the wickedness of the wicked upon their heads and He can send evil against a wicked person in order to give the person a taste of his or her own medicine. This is why He said through His Apostles, **"Be not deceived; God is not mocked: for whatsoever a man soweth, that shall he also reap"** (Galatians 6:7).

Therefore, if you sow evil, He will make sure that He gives it to you in return. How else is He going to be able to judge the world if He cannot do all these things? This is one of the reasons why Jesus said, **"With God all things are possible"** (Matthew 19:26).

God again tells us in **Isaiah 45:11-12** that He is the creator of the earth, man, the heavens and all of their hosts as you can see below:

> "Thus saith the LORD, the Holy One of Israel, and his Maker, **Ask me of things to come concerning my sons, and concerning the work of my hands command ye me.** *12* <u>**I have made the earth, and created man upon it: I, even my hands, have stretched out the heavens, and all their host have I commanded...**</u>"

What God is saying is that **if you want to know anything about Him or His creation that you should <u>ask</u> Him** (command me means ask me). In other words, ask me to tell you about me, my children, my creation or the works of my hands. **If people were to turn to the Lord and ask Him questions about Him and His creation as He has instructed us in the scripture above, all the crazy theories about the origin of man and the universe will be resolved. Many scholars will not continue to postulate atheistic or agnostic theories as they currently do.**

The unfortunate thing is that many people claim to know too much and to know more than the God who created them. Therefore, many atheists and agnostics arrogantly parade their ignorance in the form of scientific facts about God, His creation and His ways. They do not humble themselves to ask God with faith about what they need to know that He is ready and willing to teach them. God is a Father and a Teacher to those who humble themselves before Him and He will teach you about the secret things of life when you ask Him or when He sees that you desire to know them from Him.

A very good example is the King Nebuchadnezzar who was not a Jew or a Christian and who practiced idolatry but **he had a genuine desire to know how this whole world will one day end**. God in His willingness, revealed it to him in a dream. Today, even the Church of Jesus Christ is still trying to get a better understanding of this dream that God gave to a heathen king thousands of years ago. We see this in **Daniel 2:28-29:**

> "But there is a **God in heaven that revealeth secrets, and maketh known to the king Nebuchadnezzar what shall be in the latter days**. Thy dream, and the visions of thy head upon thy bed, are these; *29* **As for thee, O king, <u>thy thoughts came into thy mind upon thy bed, what should come to pass hereafter</u>** *(the end times)*: **and <u>he that revealeth secrets</u>** (God) <u>**maketh known to thee what shall come to pass**</u>."

As you can clearly see, God answered King Nebuchadnezzar's thought about the end of time. Always remember that God said, "Ask me concerning the works of my hands; **command ye Me**." He even told the skeptics to "ask" Him concerning His sons (children)." Therefore, if an unbeliever wants to know about Christians, let him or her go to the Lord and ask Him for information or knowledge. When you go to **Isaiah 45:18-23**, you will see Him telling everyone to come to Him and not to turn to any other entity for worship because beside Him there is no God:

> "**For thus saith the LORD that created the heavens; God himself that formed the earth and made it; he hath established it, he created it not in vain, he formed it to be inhabited:** <u>I am the LORD; and there is none else. *19* I have not spoken in secret, in a dark place of the earth: I said not unto the seed of Jacob, Seek ye me in vain: I the LORD speak righteousness, I declare things that are right.</u>

> *20* **Assemble yourselves and come; draw near together, ye that are escaped of the nations: they have no knowledge that set up the wood of their graven image, and pray unto a god that cannot save.** *21 (to the skeptics and idolaters He says)* **Tell ye, and bring them near; yea, let them take counsel together: who hath declared this from ancient time? who hath told it from that time? have not I the LORD? and there is no God else beside me; a just God and a Saviour;** <u>there is none beside me.</u>

> *22* <u>Look unto me, and be ye saved, all the ends of the earth: for I am God, and there is none else.</u> *23* <u>I have sworn by myself, the word is gone out of my mouth in righteousness, and</u>

**shall not return, That unto me every knee shall bow, every tongue shall swear**."

He is still telling humanity; don't seek for another God because you are not going to find it, I am it. I alone can save you, I am a Righteous Judge, I am your Savior; Jehovah and I am your provider. Every knee will bow before Him on the last day whether the knees like it or not. There will be no escaping Him on Judgment Day. You heard Him in the above scriptures that this is how it is going to go down on Judgment Day –every knee bowing to Him!

# Chapter 2
# Knowing Who God the Father Is

## How God Wants to Be Known

As I stated earlier, God wants us to always remember that He is God and that there is none else besides Him and I believe that He gave the man Moses vital keys about how He wants us to know Him. When it was time for God to bring about His plan of salvation of man into the earth realm, He looked for a man and He found that man in Abraham. Therefore, He initially dealt with Abraham, then with Isaac and Jacob and down the road in Exodus; He began to deal with Moses.

Although Abraham, Isaac and Jacob knew God, what you are going to see as we look at Moses' relationship and walk with God is that Moses came to know God most intimately. His knowledge of God went beyond that of all those that were before him. Moses came on the scene totally ignorant of who God was but out of curiosity, he had an encounter with God by the burning bush and this began his relationship with God.

**Moses was not a particularly religious person as defined by the Jewish customs of his days because he grew up in the house of Pharaoh and he was instructed in all the ways of Egypt. He knew all the Egyptian ways of worship and customs but the God of Abraham, Isaac and Jacob was unknown to him.** He was actually minding his own business in the woods when he suddenly saw a bush burning and he went to check it out. He was amazed at the fact that the bush was burning but it was not being consumed so his curiosity got the best of him and he went to investigate it. The Bible says that when God saw that Moses turned aside to look at the bush, God spoke to him as recorded in **Exodus 3:1-4:**

> "Now Moses kept the flock of Jethro his father
> in law, the priest of Midian: and he led the

flock to the backside of the desert, and came to the mountain of God, even to Horeb. 2 And the angel of the LORD appeared unto him in a flame of fire out of the midst of a bush: and he looked, and, <u>behold, the bush burned with fire, and the bush was not consumed</u>. 3 **And Moses said, I will now turn aside, and see this great sight, why the bush is not burnt.** 4 <u>**And when the LORD saw that he turned aside to see**</u>**, God called unto him out of the midst of the bush,** and said, Moses, Moses..."

Moses grew up seeing things from an Egyptian perspective and at one point, he did not even know that he was in any way connected to the Jews or that they were part of his heritage. He had seen Egyptians oppressing the Jews over the years as he was growing up and it meant nothing to him until he was about forty and he learned that he was in fact, the son of a Jew! When he realized his true heritage, he had a change of heart concerning the Jews and he began to have sympathy for the Jews; to the point that he took it upon himself to become the avenger of the Jews by killing an Egyptian who was grievously smiting a Jew. Moses got into trouble with Pharaoh for this and he went on the run to Midian. While in Midian, He had a rage against the God of the Hebrews for allowing "His chosen people" to be afflicted so grievously in Egypt without doing anything to help or deliver them.

What Moses wanted to know was, if the Jews were truly God's chosen people and they were faithfully serving Him, why would such a God leave them in such great bondage and such hardship and not do anything to help them? Therefore, Moses' rage against the God of the Jews made him desire to find this God and ask Him what the Jewish people did to Him to make Him abandon them. In other words, his heart's desire was to meet with this God so that he can give Him a piece of his mind concerning His dealings with the children of Israel.

I only know this fact about Moses because some years ago, God the Father literally walked into my bedroom and He talked with me for about 5 hours without taking a breath! According to Him, He came to answer my raging questions against Him concerning my people; black people. He said that I too desired to ask Him about slavery and His seemingly lack of regard for what happens to black people all over the world. In other words, He said that just like Moses, I was looking for Him to ask Him what we black people did to Him to leave us to such a wicked fate and not do anything about it. **He told me that He visited me for the same reasons that He visited Moses because we both had the same rage against Him concerning the sufferings of our people!**

Just like Moses, when I think about colonialism in Africa and what the Africans were subjected to in their homelands and when I also read about the slavery and the afflictions, degradations and the unspeakable inhumane treatments that black people suffered as slaves and ex-slaves in Europe, America, the Caribbean, etc., I was equally enraged. When I especially began to encounter racism, and when I saw the differences in the way that black people were being treated from the grocery stores to the workplaces, I too judged God as having been unfair to us blacks. I was looking for Him so that I could give Him a piece of my mind as well. Before my salvation, I used to verbalize my rage against Him and according to Him, He saw me.

My question to Him also was, **"What did we do to Him as black people in Africa and everywhere else in the world that He lets other races oppress, enslave and mistreat us the way that they do and not do anything about it?"** Again, in God's words, this rage against Him was what Moses and I had in common. We were looking for Him not because we wanted to praise or worship Him. The truth of the matter is, we did not know Him from Adam but we had a desire to meet with Him because we had very strong feelings concerning the injustice against our people and we both held Him responsible for it.

As a result, He came to set the record straight with us. With Moses, God sent him to Egypt to be the agent of the deliverance that Moses so desired to see for his people but with me and "all the ignorant people like me" that have been judging Him based on what we see, He had some questions. He demanded that I and all the "know-it-alls" answer His questions just as He demanded answers from the man Job and He spoke for 5 hours without taking a breath! It was like living the book of Job with all the questions that He demanded answers for. According to Him, all who question God or think that they know too much should answer the questions in the book of Job.

From what He told me, it may seem as though Moses "stumbled" upon God, but what Moses did not know was that God actually picked him from his mother's womb to fulfill God's call upon his life. The call was for him to be Israel's deliverer from their bondage in Israel! His raging desires against God only helped to propel him to where he could have an encounter with God. His meeting with God at the burning bush was actually a divine appointment by God. **During the encounter, God formally introduced Himself to Moses.** We see this in **Exodus 3:6** as God says to Moses:

> "Moreover **he** *(God)* **said, I am the <u>God of thy father</u>, the God of Abraham, the God of Isaac, and the God of Jacob.** And Moses hid his face; for he was afraid to look upon God."

Remember that Moses was not really a part of the Jewish community in Egypt. He was a wanted man in Egypt for killing an Egyptian who was grievously smiting a Jew. **The fact of the matter is that he never really lived with the Jews while he was in Egypt. Also, the Jews did not regard him as one of them and they had a distrust of him because he was genuinely a Prince of Egypt**. Therefore, when God told him to go back to Egypt as a "Deliverer" of the Jews, he asked for help from God because he knew that the people will not believe that God met with him.

You can see his limited knowledge of who the God of the Hebrews is because he asked God in **Exodus 3:13-15, "What is your name?"** Again, this shows us just how ignorant Moses was about the identity of the God of Israel. He did not even know the name that the Israelites called their God. Most Jews in Egypt at the time knew the name of God:

> "And Moses said unto God, **Behold, when I come unto the children of Israel, and shall say unto them, The God of <u>your fathers</u> hath sent me unto you; and they shall say to me, What is his name? <u>what shall I say unto them?</u> 14 And God said unto Moses, I AM THAT I AM: and he said, Thus shalt thou say unto the children of Israel, I AM hath sent me unto you.**

> 15 And God said moreover unto Moses, **Thus shalt thou say unto the children of Israel, The <u>LORD God</u> of your fathers, <u>the God of Abraham</u>, <u>the God of Isaac</u>, and <u>the God of Jacob</u>, hath sent me unto you: <u>this is my name for ever</u>, and <u>this is my memorial unto all generations</u>.**"

Why would God say this about how He wants to be known forever as a perpetual memorial? God being **All-Knowing** already foresaw that there would be a group of people today; billions of them as a matter of fact, who would be **worshipping the God of Abraham and the God of Ishmael** through the Islamic religion. Therefore, He tells us through Moses how He wants to be known and remembered forever –**the God of Abraham, the God of Isaac and the God of Jacob. Although Ishmael and Isaac were both the sons of Abraham, God sovereignly chose to place the blessings of salvation and the**

**right of inheritance in Isaac and not Ishmael because Isaac was the legitimate son by Abraham's wife while Ishmael was the son of a bond woman (a slave) –great difference between the children.** Therefore, the Judeo God of Abraham, Isaac and Jacob that we worship in Christendom today is not the same God that the Ishmaelites are worshipping through the Islamic religion.

**Again, they are worshipping the God of Abraham and Ishmael** but we must always remember that the blessing is in Isaac and not in Ishmael. **Moreover, God personally told us in the scriptures above how He wants to be known and remembered forever as a perpetual memorial of Him.** Therefore, you must know Him and worship Him accordingly. **When you come to God, you must know Him as the God of Abraham, the God of Isaac, and the God of Jacob so that you can receive the covenant blessings that He placed in Isaac through Abraham.**

## God as the Almighty

God said something really interesting in **Exodus 6:3** when He said to Moses:

> "...I appeared unto Abraham, unto Isaac, and unto Jacob, by the name of <u>God Almighty</u>, but by my name <u>JEHOVAH</u> was I not known to them."

God Almighty means **El Shaddai** –the **All-Sufficient One** and also the **One who provides**. What God is saying here is that Abraham, Isaac and Jacob only knew Him as their **Provider**. They knew that He is sufficient to meet their needs and He did. They knew how to offer sacrifices to Him and they knew how to ask Him for things. Therefore, they only knew Him as God Almighty but they did not know Him as **Jehovah** which means the **Self-Existing One** or **the Eternal One**.

In the days of Abraham, Isaac and Jacob, man's needs were very basic; therefore, their primary daily desires were for provisions and protection from all harm. It is the reason that they only knew God as a provider and a protector but today, if you only know God as your provider (i.e., on the level of meeting your needs), you will not be able to live a successful Christian life of overcoming your spiritual adversaries. Because life on earth has become more complex, you will be selling yourself short of the higher place that He has called you to know Him in Christ. Because of our new birth in Christ, we now have better promises in the New Testament than the children of Israel had in the Old Testament. It is the reason that the Lord Jesus declared the following in **Matthew 11:11**:

> "Verily I say unto you, **Among them that are born of women** <u>there hath not risen a greater than John the Baptist</u>: **notwithstanding he that is least in the kingdom of heaven is greater than he.**"

The key here is that **John was born of a woman** but **we** (the Born Again Christians) **are born of the Spirit of God**. Great difference! This is why we are sons and daughters of God by our new birth.


## God as the Self-Existing One or the Eternal One

What does it mean to know God as the **Self-Existing One** or the **Eternal One**? Knowing God as the **Self-Existing One** will again take us to the beginning when He was talking about Himself in **Isaiah 45. He informed us that from the beginning that He has always been or has always existed and that from eternity unto eternity, there is no other God besides Him.** He is the **Self-Existing One** who created all things that currently exist and He is more than able to be whatever man needs.

Again, because man's needs have become so complex in today's society, you must know Him as the **Self-Existing**

**One**. Why do you think that He introduced Himself to Moses thus? Because, as the **Eternal One** or the **Self-Existing One**, His abilities go beyond just being our provider, our peace, our rest, our defender, and whatever else we need Him to be. Therefore, you can say here that He gave Moses a broader perspective about Himself and about His abilities. This is what He said about Himself in this regard in **Jeremiah 32:27**:

> "<u>Behold, I am the LORD, the God of all flesh</u>: **is there anything too hard for me?**"

He wants us to know that as the **Self-Existing One**, He needs nothing outside of Himself to be whatever we want Him to be or to do whatever we will ever want Him to do because **with Him, all things are possible!** There is nothing that He cannot do and there is no where that His awesome right hand cannot reach. We must therefore be fully persuaded that truly His abilities do go beyond meeting our needs and sustaining us.

For example, when the children of Israel needed deliverance from the Egyptian bondage and enslavement, He raised up Moses for them as their **Deliverer** and through Moses provided them with what they needed in and out of Egypt. In **Exodus 3:14**, He wanted Moses and all of us to also know Him as the **I AM** when He said to Moses, **"Tell them that I AM THAT I AM has sent me unto you." As the I AM, there is no limit to what He can do.** I will discuss knowing God as the **I AM THAT I AM** later in Chapter 5 of this book.

The children of Israel on the other hand, knew Him only on the level of Provider and their basic attitude was, "Give me bread and if I don't get it, I will murmur and I will complain." To them, He was just a Provider and whenever He did not provide what they needed on time, they could not exercise faith in His eternal and limitless abilities. As I stated in one of my sermons titled, **"How to Move God's Heart,"** murmuring and complaining prolongs a person's wilderness experience just like the children of Israel. What happened to the children of Israel that came out of Egypt murmuring and complaining all the time? They all perished in the wilderness except for two: Caleb and Joshua.

Caleb and Joshua were the only ones that trusted in the **Eternal One** or **the Self-Existing One** that can make anything happen; even if it means that He has to create it. They trusted God to give them victory in their battles against their enemies. The rest of the camp refused to know Him as such but out of fear of their enemies blamed Moses for taking them out of Egypt. Today, a lot of Christians that only know God as the **Almighty** (the one who provides for them), are not different from the children of Israel in the wilderness who also murmured and complained when their needs were not met on time.

Also, if you do not know God as the **Self-Existing One**, but are resting in the place of knowing Him as your provider, you run the risk of falling the way that Adam fell. According to God's rule, everyone gets tested; all who will live godly must suffer persecution and you want to stand and not fall when you are tested. **Adam did not know God by His Word and so when the Word of God that came to him was tested, he fell.** Therefore, you do not want to fall when the devil sends circumstances or people to challenge the Word of God over your life. Many people have left the Christian faith as a result of some offence or some circumstance that they blame God or other Christians for. You learn obedience to God's Word and you are established in your Christian walk by God through testing. **Hebrews 12:5-11** attests to this truth:

> "And ye have forgotten the exhortation which speaketh unto you as unto children, My son, despise not thou the chastening of the Lord, nor faint when thou art rebuked of him: 6 **For**

**whom the Lord loveth he chasteneth, and scourgeth every son whom he receiveth.** *7* **If ye endure chastening, God dealeth with you as with sons;** for what son is he whom the father chasteneth not?

*8* **But if ye be without chastisement, whereof all are partakers, then are ye bastards, and not sons.** *9* Furthermore we have had fathers of our flesh which corrected us, and we gave them reverence: shall we not much rather be in subjection unto the Father of spirits, and live?

*10* **For they verily for a few days chastened us after their own pleasure; but he for our profit, that we might be partakers of his holiness.** *11* Now no chastening for the present seemeth to be joyous, but grievous: nevertheless afterward it yieldeth the peaceable fruit of righteousness unto them which are exercised thereby."

## Moses Hungered to Behold God's Glory

Moses had a great desire to have an in-depth knowledge of God and so, he pressed in for a deeper revelation of who God is to him. Moses did something that was very interesting; **he requested to behold the glory of the Lord**. This request led to the LORD revealing Himself to Moses in a way that He had not revealed Himself to anyone before Moses. Again, it is one of the reasons why the Bible says that **Moses knew the ways of the Lord but the children of Israel only knew His acts.** See how he petitioned God in **Exodus 33:18, "... I beseech thee, shew me thy glory."** Mind you that before this time, Moses had been having conversations and visitations from God but to him, it was not enough; he needed more.

In His response, God told Moses that He cannot see His face but that He will reveal some things about Himself to

Moses in **Exodus 33:19.** Just like Moses, we all need to know and understand these things today:

> "...I will **make all my goodness pass before thee, and** I will proclaim the name of the LORD before thee; **and will be gracious to whom I will be gracious, and will shew mercy on whom I will shew mercy.**"

From God's reply we can see that He has the following attributes:
- Goodness
- Other names besides God-Almighty and Jehovah
- He is gracious
- He is merciful

All these are aspects of God that He wants Moses to know because they will help Moses to develop a good understanding of who He is. What this means is that Moses must be well grounded in God's goodness and he must also learn what each of God's names mean. He needs be acquainted with how gracious God can be and also with what His limits are. In other words, Moses must learn about God's mercy as well as know the point at which God's mercy gives way to His judgment. Continuing on in **Exodus 33:20-23**, God says:

> "**And he said, Thou canst not see my face: for** there **shall no man see me, and live.** 21 And the LORD said, Behold, there is a place by me, and **thou shalt stand upon a rock**: 22 And it shall come to pass, while my glory passeth by, that **I will put thee in a clift of the rock, and will cover thee with my hand while I pass by**: 23 And I will take away mine hand, and thou shalt see my back parts: **but my face shall not be seen**."

There is something that I want to say about the scripture above. Although it is not part of the topic at hand, I think that it needs to be said because it will show us something about the ways of God and it will also help us appreciate what He did for us in Christ. It has to do with what He revealed to me concerning this particular scripture above. I danced around for days after He revealed to me this truth that I am about to share with you.

One of my testimonies is that seven months after my salvation, God the Father walked into my bedroom and talked with me from 1 am to 6 am. He answered a lot of the questions that I had concerning Him, His Son and His kingdom. As soon as He left, another entity (the devil) also came into my bedroom and the first thing that he said to me concerning the visitation by God the Father was, "No man shall see God and live!"

With those words, he threw my life into a whirlwind of panic attacks and what was supposed to be a very pleasant and happy memory for me about God the Father's visitation became a crisis for how I was going to survive after beholding the face of God the Father. Because I was newly born again at the time, I thought that the entity was right and that I was truly going to die because I beheld the face of God. This was one of the devil's initial attempts to deceive me by giving me the misinterpretation of the scripture above.

As a result, I am very familiar with the misinterpretation of this scripture. Many people have been frightened away from seeking the face of God because of this misinterpretation. You can see why it was very necessary for the Lord to help me to understand what He said and to distinguish it from what some people are saying that is a part of their misinterpretations. As for me, my survival was at stake because I needed to know if I was truly going to die as a result of God the Father visiting me. Therefore, He took me to the scripture above and He helped me to understand both its context and its meaning. Below is what He taught me.

To begin with, what is God talking about when He said, **"<u>THERE</u> shall no man see me and live?"** I want you to know that God was talking about a physical place—the tabernacle that Moses built. When you read **Exodus 33:7-8, you will see that** Moses had set up a tabernacle outside the camp where he goes to talk with God. Therefore, when God said **THERE**, He is referring to Moses' physical and spiritual location or positions regarding salvation. This is why He immediately informed Moses of the safe place where Moses can see His backside but he cannot see the face of God and live.

God said to Moses, because you have found favor in my sight I am going to put you in the **cleft of the rock** and I am going to show you a special grace. I am going to cover you with my hand and when I take away my hand and you shall see my backside but you shall not see my face. Moses has been walking very closely with God but he had never seen God's face and as a result of his spiritual and physical location (not born again) during this conversation, he would die if he saw God's face because of his "sin nature." In other words, Moses was not yet recreated in Christ Jesus the Rock and therefore cannot behold God's glorious face. This is why the Lord Jesus said in **John 3:3**:

> "Jesus answered and said unto him, **Verily, verily, I say unto thee, Except a man be born again, he cannot <u>see</u> the kingdom of God.**"

Again, what God was saying to Moses was, <u>because of where you are spiritually and physically, you cannot even behold my glory</u> (face) but I will hide you in a rock so that I can let you see my backside as my glory passes before you.

Today, there is a fallacy in Christendom in the blanket statement that if you see God, you are going to die period. But, when you look at the scripture again, you will see that God quickly told Moses, **"Behold, there is <u>a place by me,</u>**

and <u>thou shalt stand upon a rock</u>." Therefore, it is not true that everyone who sees God will die. Those who see God and live to tell about it are BORN AGAIN CHRISTIANS whom God has placed in the cleft of the ROCK which is Jesus Christ! Christians can behold the face of God today and for all of eternity.

As for Moses, although God placed him in the cleft of the rock and placed His hands over Moses to shield Moses, still God only showed him His backside! Why? As I just said above, the Lord Jesus gave us the answer when He said, **"Except a man be born again, he cannot see the kingdom of God"** (John 3:3). Moses was not yet born again so, he could not behold the glory of God that he asked for. He saw only the backside of God but in contrast to Moses, we that are born again have the glory of God bestowed upon us at our new birth in Christ. In other words, we have been given the honor as joint-heirs with Christ to behold the face of God the Father, to talk with Him, to represent Him on earth, to speak as His mouth-piece, as well as fellowship with Him. Also, the Lord Jesus said in **John 17:22-24** that He wants us to **behold His glory.** In the same scripture we saw that Jesus and His Father are one and that we are in Him:

> "**And <u>the glory which thou gavest me I have given them</u>;** that they may be one, even as we are one: 23 I in them, and thou in me, that they may be made perfect in one; and that the world may know that thou hast sent me, and hast loved them, as thou hast loved me. 24 **Father, I will that they also, whom thou hast given me, be with me where I am; <u>that they may behold my glory</u>, which thou hast given me:** for thou lovedst me before the foundation of the world."

Where are we Christians seeing God today? We are in the **cleft of the ROCK**; are we not? There is a place where you can see God and live to tell about it. **All those who are not in Christ will never see the face of God.** They will never behold His glory nor will they stand before Him on Judgment Day. The reason is because if they were to stand before God the Father in their "sin nature" (meaning without being recreated in Christ), their "sin nature" will cause them to combust at the presence of a very Holy God.

God cannot stand sin neither can sin stand before Him. This is why the Lord Jesus informed us that the Father has committed all judgments to Him **(John 5:27)**. After the Lord has judged the world and put down all rebellion, He will then present us all who believed in Him as well as the kingdom to His Father so that the Father will have preeminence in all things –**1 Corinthians 15:24-28**:

> "Then cometh the end, when he *(Jesus)* shall have delivered up the kingdom to God, even the Father; when he shall have put down all rule and all authority and power. 25 For he must reign, till he hath put all enemies under his feet. 26 The last enemy that shall be destroyed is death. 27 For he hath put all things under his feet. But when he saith all things are put under him, it is manifest that he is excepted *(God the Father)*, which did put all things under him. 28 **And when all things shall be subdued unto him, then shall the Son also himself be subject unto him that put all things under him, <u>that God may be all in all</u>.**"

Continuing the discussion on the ROCK and as you have seen, there is a difference between those who are born again that dwell spiritually in the cleft of the ROCK and those who are not yet born again. This is why the Bible says that we that are in Christ are called and ordained to have our spiritual eyes opened into the realm of the spirit to behold God the Father, to behold the Lord Jesus and to behold the Lord Holy Spirit.

As you see into the spiritual realm, you become privileged to see how the Lord functions inside of the Holy of Holies as our High Priest. It is a glorious sight to see how as our ROCK, He personally carries us inside of Him into the Holy of Holies before His Father!

**No one can get into the Holy of Holies by themselves; even when you see yourself inside of the Holy of Holies; it is because the Lord has carried you in Himself into it.** This is what He was trying to make us understand when He said that He was **the door of the sheep in John 10:7-9:**

> "**Verily, verily, I say unto you, <u>I am the door of the sheep</u>.** *8* **All that ever came before me are thieves and robbers: but the sheep did not hear them.** *9* **<u>I am the door: by me if any man enter in</u>, <u>he shall be saved</u>, <u>and shall go in and out</u>, <u>and find pasture</u>."**

Again He told us that He is the **way to the Father** in **John 14:6:**

> "I am the **<u>way</u>** and I am the **<u>truth</u>** and I am the **<u>life</u>, and no man come to the Father but <u>by Me</u>."**

If you notice, He did not say **<u>through Me</u>** but **<u>by Me</u>** because as He told us, He is the very **<u>door</u>** to the Father. Know therefore that whenever you see yourself going in and out of the Holy of Holies or before God the Father, you are actually doing it inside of Christ. The only way you can stand before the Father is inside of Christ and it is the only way that any man will ever be able to see God. **No one sees the Father except that the person be in His Son.**

Also, every revelation that we receive from God today is given to us by the Lord through the Holy Spirit. The Lord

Jesus is the one that gives revelations to us to help us know His Father by the Holy Spirit. He told us this Himself in **Matthew 11:27:**

> "All things are delivered unto me of my Father: <u>and no man knoweth the Son, but the Father;</u> **neither knoweth any man the Father, save the Son, and <u>he to whomsoever the Son will reveal him</u>.**"

Apart from Jesus, you cannot have any dealings with the Father. You can only see the Father because you are inside of Christ — **"For as many of you as have been baptized into Christ have put on Christ"**(Galatians 3:27). Once the Lord showed me a vision of how we that are born again are literally inside of Him when we are baptized into Him.

### Vision 1: Being In Christ
*I saw the Lord standing and holding up His hands in posture of the "Praying Hands." As I looked closely, I noticed that as He was standing with His hands raised in a prayer form, millions and millions of people from all the nations of the world were fast entering into Him at lightning speed. I watched as He was standing and receiving these millions and millions of people into Himself but I was shocked that His size remained the same. He never became enlarged because of the millions and millions of people that were entering into Him. I remember saying to Him, "Wow, Lord, we are truly inside of You" and He said, **"Yes, it is by Me that you go in to see and be with My Father."** He is the one that carries us in Himself to the Father into the Holy of Holies.*

### Vision 2: Entering the Holy of Holies
*In the second vision, I saw the Lord as our High Priest wearing a prayer shawl as He was entering into the Holy*

*of Holies. I noticed that I could look right into the inside of Him as He entered. He knew that I was curious about us being inside of Him so He wanted me to see how He carries us in Himself into the Holy of Holies. It was a most glorious sight to see us inside of Him. He is our door into the Holy of Holies. There is no other door that can take a person into the Holy of Holies.*

I wanted to share these visions with you so that you will know what it takes to enter into the Holy of Holies where the Father dwells and what it takes to behold God's face (glory) in the Holy of Holies. All Christians should therefore take delight in what God has done for us in His Son Jesus Christ.

**Always remember that Moses asked for it and never got it but we who are in Christ can freely behold the glory (face) of God in our daily lives. He granted us this grace and honor in Christ before we even became saved! This is why you can get a picture (vision) of God the Father, you can get a picture of the Lord Jesus, and you can get a picture of the Holy Spirit because of our position in Jesus Christ.** We are born of God's Spirit, we are bone of the Lord Jesus' bones, we are flesh of His flesh and we are one spirit with Him. We are God's heirs and joint-heirs with Christ. It does not get any better than this.

Coming back to Moses' request to behold God's glory, you can now see that the place and position that Moses was in at the time of his conversation with God did not permit God to reveal His glory to him because God's glory would have consumed Moses. You can also see the length to which God Himself went to in order to protect Moses so that Moses can have a glimpse of God's backside.

# *Chapter 3*
# What God's Names Reveal to Us about Him

## Knowing Him as God

To teach me about the importance of His name as **God**, the Lord took me to the book of **Genesis.** In Genesis you see the importance of God's names and how He functions under His various names. **As I stated before, God is the name and title under which He creates but He wants us to know Him deeper than that. Therefore, Genesis Chapters 1, 2 and 3 have the keys to how God wants you and me to know Him because however we know Him is how He is going to operate in our lives.** Let us begin from **Genesis 1:1-31:**

> "In the beginning **God created** the heaven and the earth. 2 And the earth was without form, and void; and darkness was upon the face of the deep. And the Spirit of God moved upon the face of the waters. 3 **And God said,** Let there be light: and there was light. 4 **And God saw** the light... and God divided the light from the darkness. 5 **And God called** the light Day... 6 **And God said,** Let there be a firmament... 7**And God made** the firmament... 8 **And God called** the firmament Heaven... 9 **And God said,** Let the waters under the heaven be gathered together ...

> 26 **And God said,** Let us make man in our image, after our likeness: **and let them have dominion** <u>over the fish of the sea, and over the fowl of the air, and over the cattle, and **over all the earth**, and over every creeping thing that creepeth upon the earth.</u> 27 **So God created man** in his own image, in the image of God created he him; male and female created he them**...** 31 **And God saw** everything that he had made, and, behold,

it was very good. And the evening and the morning were the sixth day."

As you can clearly see above, the book of Genesis begins with, "In the Beginning **God** created..." because **God** has always existed from the **dateless past**; meaning the **beginning** and He operated by the title and name, **GOD**. This is why you will notice that **from Genesis 1:3**, all you see is <u>**GOD said**</u> and <u>**GOD saw**</u> and this continued until **Genesis 2:3**. You can actually use a pen to underline all the references to <u>**GOD said**</u> and <u>**GOD saw**</u> beginning from verses 3 to the end of **Genesis Chapter 1**.

The reason for this is because **GOD** is the name and title under which He operated before He made the heaven and the earth and before He made Adam. The Jews refer to Him under this title as **Elohim**. I will talk about this in detail later in the next chapter but first, let us look at the other names that He revealed to Moses because they will help claify our discussion of Him as God. They hold vital keys.

## God Pronounces His Names to Moses

God has various other names that He revealed to us while He was talking with Moses. These names are equally critical in knowing Him. In **Exodus 34:5-7**, He informed Moses that He was going to proclaim His own names before Moses as He passed by Moses. My question was why did God rattle off His names to Moses?

Have you ever met some very prideful people and noticed how they rattle off their titles and academic degrees to you or how they drop names of "important or famous people" to you? I know that God is not prideful therefore I wondered what it meant for God to proclaim His own names before Moses. I remember reading this in the scripture below and because I did not know what God was doing by proclaiming His own names before Moses, I did not know what to make of it:

"And the LORD descended in the cloud, and stood with him there, and **proclaimed the name of the LORD.** 6 And the LORD passed by before him, and proclaimed, **The LORD, The LORD God, merciful and gracious, longsuffering, and abundant in goodness and truth,** 7 **Keeping mercy for thousands, forgiving iniquity and transgression and sin,** and **that will by no means clear the guilty; visiting the iniquity of the fathers upon the children,** and **upon the children's children, unto the third and to the fourth generation.**"

Because of the questions that I had, I said to the Lord, **"Father, I know that You are not prideful; so why did you proclaim your own names before Moses? I do not know you to be one who would toot His own horn."** He said to me, **"That is what you think; that I am tooting my own horn, but I tell you that if you do not know me by these names, you can think that you are walking with Me all your life and still fall short because you do not really know Me."** He then showed me how that knowing Him by these names was what made the difference between Moses and the rest of the children of Israel!

**He told Moses the secret about Himself and about knowing Him—His Names!** His names are part of the major secrets to knowing Him. God wanted Moses and all humanity to know Him by His names. Only He can by His Spirit reveal the secret of His names to those who hunger and thirst to know Him deeper. Therefore, you must have a hunger and a thirst so that He can reveal the mystery of His names to you. He needs to see that you are hungry and thirsty for more of Him just as Moses was. Below is an example of how God responded to Moses because Moses knew His name. This is the type of hunger He is looking for:

> "Because he hath set his love upon me,
> therefore will I deliver him: <u>I will set him on
> high, because he hath known my name</u>. *15*
> He shall call upon me, and I will answer him:
> I will be with him in trouble; I will deliver
> him, and honour him. *16* With long life will
> I satisfy him, and shew him my salvation"
> (Psalm 91:14-16).

Let us see how God's name and title changed from God to
LORD God.

## Knowing Him as LORD God

At the beginning of this chapter, we saw God's name as
**God** from **Genesis 1:1 to Genesis 2:3** but beginning from
**Genesis 2:4,** we see **God** now referred to under the new name
or title of **<u>LORD God</u>. Genesis 2:4** states:

> "These are the generations of the heavens
> and of the earth when they were created, in
> the day that the <u>LORD God</u> made the earth
> and the heavens..."

We can clearly see Him now being referred to as the **LORD
God;** so what changed? Previously all the references to Him
were **<u>God</u>, <u>God</u>, <u>God</u>,** but what did He do to cause this name
change? What made Him to take on an additional name? It
is obvious that He added **LORD** to His name **God** but why?
The reason is because He has created a new being –man! **He
has created this being in His own image and after His own
likeness and He has also given the man dominion over all
the earth. This single act of giving man dominion over the
earth changed His title from God to LORD God!:**

> "And God said, **Let us make man** *(Adam)* in our
> image, after our likeness: and let them **have
> dominion** <u>over the fish of the sea</u>, and <u>over the
> fowl of the air</u>, and <u>over the cattle</u>, and **over all**

**the earth**, and <u>over every creeping thing that creepeth upon the earth</u>" (Genesis 1:26).

The earth and all that is in it are the works of God's hands and He handed it over to the man that He created in **Genesis 1:26** and **in so doing made the man Lord of the whole earth! Therefore, now, He is not just God but the Lord and the God of the man while the man is the Lord of the earth.** Since, Lucifer's rebellion and before He created Adam, He had no man <u>on earth</u> for Him to be Lord over but now that He has Adam, He became Adam's Lord and Adam's God while Adam became the Lord of everything on earth.

Because He created Adam in **Genesis 1:26, He now has sovereignty over Adam. When you are a sovereign over a group of people, you are Lord.** Hence from the above scripture you can now see the reason for the change in God's name. He moved from just being **God** to becoming the **LORD God**. Remember the names that He proclaimed before Moses in **Exodus 34:6** began with, "**The LORD, the LORD God...**"

As a result, **we have to know Him first as our God, as our LORD and as our LORD God**. There are many today that do not want to accept that He is God and there are many more that do not know Him or want Him as their **LORD**. There are some Christians that only know Him as the **Almighty** while others only know Him as **God**. They are willing to accept that He made everything and that is as far as their knowledge of Him goes. The truth of the matter is that He is **God** whether or not we like it and He is **LORD** whether or not we want to acknowledge Him as such. To make Him your LORD God on the other hand, is a personal choice or a personal decision.

Once Adam came into the picture, the first assignment God gave him was to give names to everything on earth. **Therefore, Adam immediately began to rule over everything by naming them. By doing this, Adam was making everything subject to his dominion on earth and he was reigning over the earth** but God Himself needed to operate on earth as Adam's Lord so He gave Adam instructions concerning all living things under his jurisdiction including the **"Tree of Life"** and the **"Tree of the Knowledge of Good and Evil"** as recorded in **Genesis 2:15-17:**

> **"And the LORD God took the man, and put him into the Garden of Eden to dress it and to keep it** *(Adam's dominion over the earth).* *16* **And the LORD God commanded the man, saying** *(God's dominion over Adam),* **Of every tree of the garden thou mayest freely eat:** *17* **But of the "Tree of the Knowledge of good and evil,"** thou shalt not eat of it**: for in the day that thou eatest thereof** thou shalt surely die**."**

**He wanted Adam to have the type of knowledge that produces life and to stay away from the knowledge that is mixed with a little good but has enough evil to bring about Adam's death. From this, you can see God exercising His dominion over Adam.** It is a good dominion to help Adam avoid an unseen enemy that was in the garden — the devil. God is still doing the same with us who are in Christ today because **He still wants us to stay away from the fruit of the tree that produces death.**

We all already know what Adam and his wife did with God's commandment to them. When a rebellious entity (the devil) challenged the **LORD God's** commandment to them, they obeyed him rather than obeying the **LORD God**. What they were not aware of was that the rebellious entity itself was once under God's Lordship but chose to come out from under it. As a result, he was their arch enemy and we see this in **Genesis 3:1-5:**

> "Now the serpent was more subtil than any beast of the field which the LORD God had made. And he said unto the woman, **Yea, hath**

**God said, Ye shall not eat of every tree of the garden?** *(not an accurate quote of what God said)* 2 And the woman said unto the serpent, We may eat of the fruit of the trees of the garden:

3 But of the fruit of the tree which is in the midst of the garden, God hath said, Ye shall not eat of it, neither shall ye touch it, lest ye die. 4 And the serpent said unto the woman, **Ye shall not surely die: 5 For God doth know that in the day ye eat thereof, then your eyes shall be opened, and ye shall be as gods, knowing good and evil** *(this is the evil knowledge that God wanted them to avoid)."*

In **Genesis 3:6**, we see that the fall of man from God's grace was the result of listening and yielding to a different voice instead of the Sovereign voice of his **LORD God.** The devil offered Eve a taste of the fruit of evil and she lusted after it:

**"And when the woman saw that the tree was good for food, and that it was pleasant to the eyes, and a tree to be desired to make one wise, <u>she took of the fruit thereof, and did eat</u>, and gave also unto her husband with her; <u>and he did eat</u>."**

**Adam and Eve of their own free-will chose to obey the devil and in so doing lost the dominion over the earth to the devil!** Even today, those who censor God's Word or His instructions to them are doing exactly what Adam and Eve did. They too lose ground to the devil in their lives. The rules have not changed as far as God is concerned and the devil is still out there to deceive all those who do not know their **LORD God** and His Word. This is why the Lord Jesus said in **Romans 6:16**:

**"Know ye not, that to whom ye yield yourselves <u>servants to obey</u>, <u>his servants ye are to whom</u>**

**ye obey; whether of sin unto death, or of obedience unto righteousness?"**

From all the scriptures above that we have seen so far, you can learn about how you are supposed to know **God** as your **LORD God** so that you can avoid the sin that Adam and Eve committed. He called Adam and Eve to be under His Lordship as their **LORD God** but they submitted themselves to the serpent (the devil). By doing this, they became the devil's servants instead of operating on earth as the devil's Lord to rule over him! In return, the devil became their Lord — their instruction giver and controller. He immediately began to enslave humanity and to teach man acts of evil and rebellion against God.

Because of the dominion over the earth that the devil swindled away from Adam, he had the audacity to tell the Lord Jesus while he was tempting the Lord that the kingdoms of this world and their glory **were delivered to him** in **Luke 4:5-7:**

> "And the devil, taking him up into an high mountain, **shewed unto him all the kingdoms of the world in a moment of time.** 6 And the devil said unto him, **All this power** will I **give thee, and the glory of them**: **for that is delivered unto me; and to whomsoever I will I give it**. 7 If thou therefore wilt worship me, all shall be thine."

The question is; who delivered the power (dominion) over the whole earth to him? Adam did by subjecting himself to the devil to obey him instead of obeying the commandment of his **LORD God** and instead of commanding or rebuking the serpent when it came to him through his wife. Therefore, God drove Adam and his wife out of His garden as recorded in **Genesis 3:23-24.**

I say to you therefore that it pays to know **God** not just as your **God** but as your **LORD God** also. You should purpose in your heart to always obey His every Word:

> **"Therefore the LORD God sent him forth from the garden of Eden, to till the ground from whence he was taken. 24 So he drove out the man; and he placed at the east of the garden of Eden Cherubims, and a flaming sword which turned every way, to keep the way of the tree of life."**

Today, there is still no place in God for those who choose to disregard His Word and to live as they please. He has called everyone to repent and come to Him through His Son Jesus Christ. As a result, He has Christians as His representatives on earth. Everyone on earth needs to recognize them as such and obey the Word of the Lord that comes through them.

### *Effects of Feeding From the Wrong Tree*

If Adam and Eve had eaten from the **"Tree of Life,"** they would have lived forever and they would not have fallen because the **"Tree of Life"** is the **Word of God**. The Word of God is the only thing that can keep a person from falling into the devil's trap and as long as you are feeding from it, you are not going to listen to the devil's lies. The Lord Jesus is the ultimate **Word of God** and He is the **Tree of Life**; everyone that feeds on Him (His Word) has life and everyone that does not, has no life.

Adam and Eve were not eating from any tree and so the devil saw in them a vacuum and he said to himself, "I will go and feed them the wrong food because they will not know the difference and neither will they know it's devastating effects." When you are constantly feeding on the Word of God, you will recognize when an error comes to you and you will not go for it. This is why a lot of people are deceived today because they do not know the Word of God so they can easily buy into lies and deceits.

Also, there are some individuals out there preaching all types of strange doctrines that sound religious; they sound holy but they are not exactly according to the Word of the Lord. Many of them have teamed up with "New Age Doctrines" and they twist these "New Age Doctrines" to fit their purposes. Their words may sound "noble" and they may "seem" to have "good intentions" but when you test them with the Word of the Lord, you will discover that they are doctrines of devils.

This is why we that are Christians are not called to live by somebody else's good intentions or what seems good in our eyes but by the Word of the Lord. Many people have followed some seemingly "good leaders with good intentions" to their own destructions. Examples of which are Jim Jones and David Koresh.

Today, their history represents biblically ignorant people who insist on continuing to eat the fruit of the "Tree of the Knowledge of good and evil" and who continue to sell it to others. They do not care about the people that they are deceiving as long as their desires or lusts are met. The Lord Jesus called such people children of the devil in **John 8:44:**

> **"Ye are of your father the devil, and the lusts of your father ye will do. He was a murderer from the beginning, and abode not in the truth, because there is no truth in him.** When he speaketh a lie, he speaketh of his own: **for he is a liar, and the father of it."**

Only the Word of God can keep you from being deceived by these types of people but those who do not spend time with

God and His Word are more likely to receive teachings of their lies that are mixed with a little truth (Tree of the Knowledge of good and evil) and become deceived. The devil then uses them as his children to deceive others. As I already stated, anyone that eats from the **"Tree of Life"** will know error when it comes to them. It is quite simple because when you spend time in the Bible and someone says something that is contrary to the Word of God to you, you are going to reject it.

This is why the Bible says, **"Take heed that you do not be deceived."** How do you take heed? By knowing the Word of God; it has always been the Word of God that shows us the right path. This is the reason why God wants us all to know and to live by what He said in **Deuteronomy 8:3** that:

> **"...Man does not live by bread alone but by every word that proceeds forth out the mouth of God."**

The Word of God is our life because His Words are spirit and they are life! There is no doubt that if you do not know God's Word, you can still be deceived today; thousands of years after Adam and Eve were deceived. Take a look around you; are not many people being deceived even today? Billions of people are into false religions and they are still stubbornly eating that evil fruit (the words of the devil) that God commanded man to stay away from. As a result, billions of people are worshiping all kinds of objects as "gods" because the devil has deceived them to believe his lies about life, creation, the earth and God.

### *King David and King Solomon Knew About the LORD God*
Some of the people in the Old Testament that had a personal revelation about the importance of having God in your life as the **LORD God** were prophets, King David and his son **King Solomon**. When you read about David;

especially in the Psalms, you will notice that he understood what it meant for **God** to be **LORD God** in his life. Although David himself was not yet restored in Christ (born again), he had a spiritual revelation of the meaning of God's title, the **LORD God**. Look at what he said in **1 Chronicles 29:1:**

> "Furthermore David the king said unto all the congregation, Solomon my son, whom alone God hath chosen, is yet young and tender, and the work is great: **for the palace is not for man, but for the LORD God**."

He accepted God not just as his **God** but as his **LORD**. Also, King Solomon said in **2 Chronicles 1:9:**

> "Now, **O LORD God**, let thy promise unto David my father be established: for thou hast made me king over a people like the dust of the earth in multitude."

Solomon got this revelation from his father and from his close relationship with God because the Spirit of Wisdom and Counsel were operating heavily in his life. Therefore, he had a revelation of what it means for the **LORD** to be **LORD God**.

Both David and Solomon spent time with the **LORD**; remember all the Psalms, the book of Proverbs and the intimacy that David and Solomon had with the Lord? They learned some things about the Lord; they leaned that they had to make **God** the **LORD God** over their lives. David was totally sold out to God and he was totally submitted to the **LORD** as his **God**.

God wants people to have this knowledge about Him because it makes a way for Him to help a person when the person is in need and also to guide the person through all the obstacles in life. **The Lord told me to take a look at a lot of the different countries that chose to worship idols instead of Him and to note how the devil has been able to ravage**

**them with poverty, sicknesses, diseases, lack of scientific or economic development and other things.** The reason that the devil has been so successful against these countries is because they have not accepted the Lord as their **LORD God.**

## Knowing God as the LORD

Once the **LORD God** drove away the man and his wife from His garden, His title changed again. Now, He is just **LORD** because man rejected Him as his personal **God!** A **Lord** is someone who rules or presides over an area; in this case God is **Lord** over the earth no matter what man thinks or does. This is why He declared in **Job 41:11** that everything under the whole of heaven belongs to Him:

> "...Whatsoever is under the whole heaven
> is mine."

Since the fall of Adam and Eve, He has been trying to teach man that He is not just the **Lord over the earth** but that He is man's **personal God** also. He wants man to know Him as his **personal God**.

As a matter of fact, He said in **Revelation 11:18** that He will destroy all those who destroyed His earth. As **Lord**, God cares for His earth that He created and He does not appreciate those who destroy His earth:

> "And the nations were angry, and thy wrath
> is come, and the time of the dead, that they
> should be judged, and that thou shouldest
> give reward unto thy servants the prophets,
> and to the saints, and them that fear thy name,
> small and great; **and shouldest destroy them
> which destroy the earth.**"

It is amazing that He has a day set aside for all those who destroyed the environment and the natural beauty of His creation to answer to Him.

I say again that as a result of the fall of Adam and Eve, **God** lost His title of **LORD God** because man rejected Him as his **Lord**. He lost the title because man demonstrated his refusal to be subjected to God's laws when man rebelled. This is why since the fall of man God has been reminding man that He alone is God and that there is none else. He continually communicated this through His prophets in the Old Testament with the saying, **"Thus saith the <u>LORD thy God</u>"** in His efforts to keep reminding man that He is man's **God**.

**Again, God has been patiently working to restore Himself back to being the only God that we worship, that we submit to, and that we put our trust in.** This proved to be a tough job for thousands of years until Jesus came to the earth and finished the works concerning our salvation on the Cross. Even after the finished works of Christ, many still do not want to accept Him as the **LORD** their **God**.

He does not want man to bow down to images or to create some other "gods" that cannot bring salvation and redemption to man. He alone is **LORD of the earth** whether or not anyone likes it, but to us who are Christians, He is the **LORD** our **God**. This is why we talk about having a personal relationship with Him as our **LORD God**.

You may not want to know Him as your LORD or your personal God but He wants you to. He wants you to get to know Him deeply so that you can know and obey His daily instructions and commandments for your life because only His instructions can give you eternal life. **Many people in the world do not want to know Him beyond the fact that He is God. I call them illegal occupants of the LORD God's earth.**

They may not want to know Him as their **LORD** or as their personal **God** but they will have to deal with Him on

Judgment Day **because He owns the earth and they MUST give Him an account of what they did while they were living on His earth rent free.** So, never forget that we all live on God's earth rent free but He has set aside a day on which all who lived here must become accountable to Him because He alone is the **LANDLORD** over the earth!

## Restoration of God's Title of LORD God

God's title of **LORD God** was not fully restored to Him until the finished work of Christ and it was demonstrated when the disciple named Thomas fell on His face and said, **"My Lord and my God"** in **John 20:28**. Remember that when the Lord Jesus rose from the dead and they told Thomas about it that Thomas did not believe it? He held on to his unbelief until the day the Lord appeared in the midst of the disciples and Thomas was present. In response, the Lord said to Thomas, **"Be not faithless, but believing"** in **John 20:27**. In response, Thomas said **my Lord and my God** in **John 20:26-28**:

> "And after eight days again his disciples were within, and Thomas with them: then came Jesus, the doors being shut, and stood in the midst, and said, Peace be unto you. 27 Then saith he to Thomas, Reach hither thy finger, and behold my hands; and reach hither thy hand, and thrust it into my side: and be not faithless, but believing. 28 And Thomas answered and said unto him, **My Lord and my God.**"

### *A Word of Wisdom from the LORD to Me*

The Lord said to me, "You can know me all your life as **God** but if I am not in your life as your personal **LORD that you surrender to,** then, I am not your **LORD God.**" Now you can see where Moses got the knowledge and understanding that enabled him to know **God** on a more personal level as his **LORD**. He must have said to himself, "Wait a minute, I have to press in to know **God** more and not just on the level that everyone else knows Him but on a more intimate and personal level as my **LORD**."

Moses wanted a personal relationship with **God** and this is what God has given to us in the person of His Son Jesus Christ! We can walk with Him as our LORD God all the days of our lives.

## Recap of God's Names in Genesis:

- He is **GOD,** the **Almighty** from **Genesis 1:1** to **Genesis 2:3** because He is Almighty over creation. This has been His name and title throughout eternity.

- He is the **LORD God** from **Genesis 2:4** to **Genesis 3:23** because after the creation of Adam and Eve, He became their Lord. It is the introduction of a relationship between the **Almighty** creator and His very special creation — **man**!

- He again became just the **LORD** in **Genesis 4:1** because man rejected Him as his **personal God** and chose rebellion but **GOD** is still the **Land LORD** of the earth so He began to operate under the title of **LORD**.

- The LORD Jesus restored man back to **GOD** so that He is **LORD God** again to all those who receive His finished works in Christ.

The lesson we learn from these scriptures is that our relationship with God is very real and our choices have an impact on Him.

## *Chapter 4*
# Knowing God by Names That Reveal His Nature

### Knowing that God is Love

You need to know and to understand that **God is love**. Love is the primary nature of God and **it is what made Him to do things like create the heavens, the earth and all the souls in them.** It is also what motivated Him to put together a plan of salvation for man when man willfully sinned against Him. He could have just wiped out the whole earth and forgotten about man but He did not because His nature of love would not let Him. He chose instead to send His only begotten Son into the earth to die a shameful, agonizing and slow death on the Cross for all of us sinners.

The world today has a very warped idea of what they believe love to be and it is one of the reasons that a lot of people think that they can fall in and out of love on a whim. Their definition of love is selfish; self-centered and self-serving but my hope is that we that are Christians have a good understanding of the scriptures in **1 John 4:7-10** that clearly tell us that **love is a person; the person of God:**

> "**Beloved, let us love one another: for love is of God**; and every one that loveth is born of God, and knoweth God. *8* **He that loveth not knoweth not God; <u>for God is love</u>.** *9* In this was manifested the love of God toward us, because that God sent his only begotten Son into the world, that we might live through him. *10* **Herein is love, not that we loved God, but that he loved us**, and sent his Son to be the propitiation for our sins."

A lack of proper understanding of this aspect of God's nature (knowing Him as love) makes people to believe in and search for an **"abstract love"** or an **"intangible love."** It is one of the primary reasons why marriages break up today because a lot of people cannot keep their marriage vows when they see another man or woman walking down the road and they like what they see better than what they have at home.

They start to make advances towards the man or woman and in due time will convince themselves that they are in love with the man or woman and that they are no longer in love with their spouse. What they do not realize is that they are in lust and not love. Love sacrifices and love will refrain from hurting a spouse or a loved one. As a result of these types of behavior, lust and selfishness have become widely accepted as love and many people are living very miserable lives because of it.

**I restate again that love is a person — the person of God. Therefore, you can only get true love from Him! He alone can fill you with His love for yourself, your spouse and for other people because when you receive His Son Jesus, He comes as love and He dwells in you. He then begins the task of making you into His love vessel by teaching you what love is and how to love selflessly.** His type of love is what we call **"agape love"** because **it is unconditional**. It is forever and it does not change, fade or diminish. To cultivate this type of unselfish love in you, He will take you to people and places where there is no love as He begins to use them to mold you so that His genuine love can flow out from you. He will actually plant and grow His love in you so that you can have it to give to others.

It is the reason that you cannot fall out of love with someone when you stay connected to Him. Without Him in your life, you are going to only love those who love you and only go after those that you perceive have something that you need or like. When you put it all together, it spells SELFISHNESS. It is the reason that God will try everyman's work with the fire of His love so that He can burn out all the things that were done with selfish motivations. In other words, on Judgment Day, God will only accept the things that we were motivated to do out of genuine love:

> "Every man's work shall be made manifest: for the day shall declare it, because it shall be revealed by fire; **and the fire shall try every man's work** of what sort it is" **(1 Corinthians 3:13).**

In **1 Corinthians 13:1-13**, we find great insight of how that God is love. **It outlines the attributes of God** (His character) **that He wants us to manifest in our daily lives. Remember that He wanted to make man in His own image and after His likeness** (character) in Genesis 1:26? Well, charity is the Latin word *Caritas* meaning **love**. Therefore, charity is just another word for love and if you replace the word **Charity** with **God** in **1 Corinthians 13**, you will gain a better idea of who God is when it comes to love:

> "Though I speak with the tongues of men and of angels, **and have not charity** *(God)*, **I am become as sounding brass, or a tinkling cymbal.** 2 And though I have the gift of prophecy, and understand all mysteries, and all knowledge; and though I have all faith, so that I could remove mountains, and **have not charity** *(God)*, **I am nothing.** 3 And though I bestow all my goods to feed the poor, and though I give my body to be burned, and **have not charity** *(God)*, **it profiteth me nothing.**
>
> 4 **Charity** *(God)* **suffereth long, and is kind; charity** *(God)* **envieth not; charity** *(God)* **vaunteth not itself, is not puffed up,** 5 **Doth not behave itself unseemly, seeketh not her own, is not easily provoked, thinketh no evil;** 6 **Rejoiceth**

**not in iniquity, but rejoiceth in the truth;** *7* **Beareth all things, believeth all things, hopeth all things, endureth all things.** *8* **Charity** *(God)* **never faileth**: but whether there be prophecies, they shall fail; whether there be tongues, they shall cease; whether there be knowledge, it shall vanish away.

*9* For we know in part, and we prophesy in part. *10* But when that which is perfect is come, then that which is in part shall be done away. *11* When I was a child, I spake as a child, I understood as a child, I thought as a child: but when I became a man, I put away childish things. *12* For now we see through a glass, darkly; but then face to face: now I know in part; but then shall I know even as also I am known. *13* And now abideth **faith**, **hope**, charity *(God)*, these three; but the greatest of these is **charity** *(God).*"

According to this scripture, love never fails! Therefore when you have the God kind of love, you cannot run out of it and it does not cease. We already know that God suffereth long and He actually called Himself the **Longsuffering One**. If you approach the above attributes from God's perspective, you will understand who you are dealing with when we talk about **God** being love Himself.

As love, He endures a lot from us without pouring out His judgment instantly on us. Also, He hopes for the best in us, He believes that we are capable of changing even when He is looking at us messing up, and He never fails when we need Him. God has never failed one human being on planet earth. He is ever faithful and He is an ever present help in time of trouble. He once emphatically told me that, **"There is no one on earth that has ever looked for Me with all their heart, with all their soul and with all their might that has failed to find Me."** He said, **"No, not one!"** At this,

He pounded His chest with His right hand and then raised His right index finger up in the air to stress this point.

One of the most interesting things about **God** is that although He created the earth and everything in it, He is not prideful. He is the most humble and most gentle person that I have ever seen or encountered. The Lord Jesus told us about this aspect of God when He said:

> "Take my yoke upon you, and learn of me; **for I am meek and lowly** *(humble)* **in heart:** and ye shall find rest unto your souls" (Matthew 11:29).

This is why the Lord Jesus came into the world as a meek lamb and He is still the meekest man that has ever lived on earth. For some people, when God gives them a little ministry and puts their faces on television, they think that they have arrived as they become puffed up. They start to act almighty as they allow pride to take hold of them. When you need anything from some of these people, you stand a better chance of seeing the President of the United States than you would these preachers.

In their mind, they think they are something but what they do not know is that God sees them from above and that He calls them the "superstars" in my house. He is very displeased with them and their "superior attitudes." We are to first love God and then love our neighbors not our ministries and our prestige. **Also, many ministers put their ministries first; even before their families. They forget that before the fall of man and the need to preach the message of salvation; there was the family.** The godly order therefore is God first, family next and then ministry. This is a word for the wise.

According to Him, these "superstars" make their grand entrance into service when Praise and Worship is almost over because to them, it is the little people that have to praise God and warm up the congregation before their big entrance. He asked me, **"Isn't Praise and Worship supposed to be about Me? And these same people ask Me to give them My power."** Then He whispered, **"What do you think that they are going to do with it?"** After this He shouted, **"But, I will not give it to them."**

He continued by saying that these ministers do everything else except sign autographs! Therefore if you are one of these types of ministers who stay in the waiting room until Praise and Worship is over so that you can make your grand entrance, God says you are a "superstar" and that you should not expect to see His power flow in your life or in your ministry. This is why we have too many fluffy words coming out of even very large ministries but no demonstration of God's power. Many of them hold onto the self-benefiting prosperity messages and programs.

Continuing the discussion of love, I want to reiterate that love is the one thing that the devil does not know how to relate to because he believes in tit-for-tat. When you choose the way of love, you throw the devil into chaos and he is baffled because he does not understand love. The devil uses people that he can stir up to do something ugly or mean to other people but when someone chooses not to retaliate with ugliness but love, the devil and his evil spirits get confused. This is why when you choose to respond in love, the next thing the devil does is send an instigator to you. He will then try to use this person to push your button of retaliation and provoke you to dish out ugliness to those who rise up against you.

The person might say to you, "I cannot believe they said that to you; can you imagine the way they said that to you? Are you going to just stand there and let them say these things to you? I do not take this from anyone so I suggest you rise up and defend yourself." Before you know it, the person has instigated you or provoked you into a negative reaction. Know therefore, that the devil uses instigators to scratch your wounds so that you do not go the way of love.

**As a result of this, you constantly have to remind yourself that God is love. Walking in the God kind of love is the reason that the Lord Jesus said to turn the other cheek when someone slaps you on one.** When you do that, you allow God to move on your behalf. You should never repay evil with evil because you earn points with God when you repay evil with love and you make room in the situation for God to avenge you.

Also, according to the Lord in **Romans 12:20**, when someone wrongs you and you repay them back with good, you heap coals of fire upon that person's head and you release God's hand to move on your behalf. He can then bless you for your obedience and at the same time avenge you from all those that have wronged you:

> "Therefore if **thine enemy** hunger, feed him; if he thirst, give him drink: **for in so doing thou shalt heap coals of fire on his head.**"

We see this again stated in **Proverbs 25:21-22** and we also learn that we will receive a reward from the Lord when we obey Him:

> "If thine enemy be hungry, give him bread to eat; and if he be thirsty, give him water to drink: 22 **For thou shalt heap coals of fire upon his head, and the LORD shall reward thee.**"

One of the first revelations that the Lord gave me when I first became born again was how He wages war on our behalf. He took me to **Revelation 19:11** so that I will always remember what He looks for on my part concerning any situation; He wants to see righteousness on my part so that He can rise up to defend me:

> "And I saw heaven opened, and behold a white horse; and <u>he that sat upon him was called Faithful and True</u>, and **in righteousness he doth judge and make war.**"

It is in our best interest to know that God wages war in righteousness. In order words, for Him to arise for you, He must see righteousness on your part concerning the issue or situation. He told me that **two wrongs do not make a right** so we always have to choose righteousness if we want Him to avenge us. Therefore, you always have to create a righteous condition by your choices in a matter and those righteous choices will allow God to war on your behalf.

**God will not war on behalf of any Christian who repays evil with evil.** He is love and He wants us to overcome evil with good. This is what our loving God requires from all of us. I will discuss this aspect of God in detail in the section called *Understanding the Ways of God*. In that section, you will clearly see the reason why God does not move on behalf of most people because they never create the righteous conditions that free up His awesome **Right Hand** to move on their behalf. Again, this is why the Lord told us in **Romans 12:17 to:**

> "**Recompense to no man evil for evil.** Provide things honest in the sight of all men."

And also in **Romans 12:21**:

> "**Be not overcome of evil, but overcome evil with good.**"

We are to get to know God and to receive His love but there are a lot of people that are righteous in their own eyes and their definition of love is by their own self-assessment. They say to themselves, "I am a good person, I am this, I am that…" and while they are in this mind frame, a lot of times they are judging God for not having been there when they needed Him or for not addressing certain situations the way that they wanted Him to.

They forget that this same God that we are dealing with is the **very essence of love and faithfulness.** When you squeeze Him, love is what comes out because He is love. You cannot love anyone or anything more than He does. **Put simply, you cannot out love Him because your love does not even come close to His definition of love. <u>Love is Him in person.</u>**

## Knowing that God is a Jealous God

**Jealousy** is not a word that many people want to be identified with but God's type of jealousy is different from man's jealousy. He is not jealous in the way that man is jealous because man's type of jealousy works destruction. **God's type of jealousy is His zeal to fight for you and me so that we can spend eternity with Him instead of with the devil in hell.** God can let you follow Harry Krishna, Mohammed, Buddha, atheism, or any other pagan religion if that is what you want to follow but because He created you for Himself (to spend eternity with you), He is jealously fighting the evil forces and your personal decisions that will put you in hell forever with the devil.

God is jealous over us because God loves us and He knows the things that prevent us from loving Him and from receiving His love. Therefore, He jealously tries to help us stay away from those things and from having idols in our lives. God hates idolatry because idolatry puts a road block in our relationship with Him and the devil uses it to steal God's glory in our lives:

> "<u>For thou shalt worship no other god</u>: **for the LORD, whose name is Jealous, is a jealous**

**God**: *15* Lest thou make a covenant with the inhabitants of the land, and they go a whoring after their gods, and do sacrifice unto their gods, and one call thee, and thou eat of his sacrifice" **(Exodus 34:14-15).**

God refuses to share HIS GLORY with idols and He is very jealous over the man (Adam and his descendants) that He created and gave dominion over the earth. **He loves us too much to watch the devil drag us into idolatry and eventually into hell without doing anything about it.** Therefore, He is very jealous over us and will not share us with some dumb idols whose sole goal is to drag us to hell. As for us, we are not to give our love and loyalty to idols. We see Him express this again in the following scriptures in **Exodus 20:4-6:**

> **"Thou shalt not make unto thee any graven image, or any likeness of anything that is in heaven above, or that is in the earth beneath, or that is in the water under the earth**: *5* Thou shalt not bow down thyself to them, nor serve them: **for I the LORD thy God am a jealous God,** visiting the iniquity of the fathers upon the children unto the third and fourth **generation of them that hate me;** *6* **And shewing mercy unto thousands of them that love me, and keep my commandments…"**

And also in **Isaiah 42:8:**

> "I am the LORD: that is my name: and my glory will I not give to another, neither my praise to graven images."

He wants to be the only God that we worship and exalt and we are to give Him all the glory for the good things that happen in our lives. We must acknowledge Him as our only God and praise His awesome name as stated in **Malachi 2:2:**

> **"If ye will not hear, and if ye will not lay it to heart, <u>to give glory unto my name</u>** *(worship and praise Him alone),* **saith the LORD of hosts, <u>I will even send a curse upon you, and I will curse your blessings</u>: yea, I have cursed them already, because ye do not lay it to heart."**

Idolatry unleashes God's wrath. Therefore He does not want you to idolize anything; even yourself. He knows what we all think of ourselves and He knows when a person thinks that he or she is too cute for those around them. He sees people who walk around putting others down and elevating themselves: yes, He sees the prideful and the arrogant ones as well as the selfish or the self-centered ones. He delights in abasing the proud and exalting the humble and He likes to visit places in our lives where we have set up idols in our hearts that rival Him. He comes to mess them up or to abase them.

While He is in those places in our lives, He begins to teach us that these things will actually put us in hell if we continue to let them rival Him in our lives. **He begins to teach us humility and the primary lesson that He has for all humanity which is that you must live by every word that comes out of His mouth.**

From what I have shown you in scriptures thus far, you can get some ideas of why He said, **"I the Lord your God am a jealous God."** I say again that you must know that God is very, very jealous of anything that will take you away from Him and place you in hell. He will jealously protect you from the heathen that have rejected Him in their lives because He knows that association with them will lead you to hell and not to Him. You will only become their prey as stated in **Ezekiel 36:5**:

> "Therefore **thus saith the Lord GOD; Surely in the fire of my jealousy have I spoken against the residue of the heathen**, and against all

71

Idumea, which have appointed my land into their possession with the joy of all their heart, with despiteful minds, to cast it out for a prey."

**Know also that God formed you so that your life will bring Him praise because of all the good things that He intends for you to do for others.** You are to be a testimony of His goodness. Unfortunately, not very many people ever tap into this revelation because greed and the love of money lead people to make eternally damning compromises in their lives:

**"This people have I formed for myself; they shall shew forth my praise"** (Isaiah 43:21).

God made man in His own image and He wants man's character (likeness) to also reflect who He is. Therefore, He will jealously fight for your soul not to be overtaken by evil or evil ways. He hates anything that you want to do that will at the end separate you from Him. **He knows that the devil and his demons will only lead you on a destructive path so He loves you enough to make sure that you do not destroy yourself.** This is His type of jealousy and as you can see, it is different from the human type of jealousy that brings nothing but destruction, divorce, killings, and other forms of wickedness.

**We all should be very happy that God is jealous over us with a holy jealousy.** We do not want it any other way. Very often we read on the internet or in the newspapers about an angry spouse who out of jealousy killed the spouse and himself or kills his ex-spouse and her new lover. This is not the God type of jealousy. **God's type of jealousy has a redeeming quality; it is meant to bring about a person's salvation.**

On the other hand, God will give a person their deserved reward in hell if the person refuses to receive God's love in His

Son Jesus Christ. **He is jealous over the righteous ones that have come to Him through Christ and will do everything necessary to keep them from the destruction of those who have willfully chosen the devil's evil ways.** This is why the Bible states in **1 John 3:10** that here on earth, there are children of God and there are children of the devil:

> "In this **the children of God are manifest**, and **the children of the devil**: whosoever doeth not righteousness is not of God, neither he that loveth not his brother."

Know therefore that God will put His finger to anything that rivals Him in your life and He will remove it, diminish it or kill it so that He alone has the preeminence in your life. With some people, it is their money, reputation, their prestige, their position of influence, their children, their spouse or their job that rivals God in their lives. Whichever the case, He knows how to go after them in your life in order to get you to the place where you can recognize that when you are blessed in any of these areas, you will know that it is because He has blessed you in it. As a result, you will begin to give Him the glory that He deserves in your life.

I was shocked when God revealed to me some of the things that had rivaled Him in my life. Below is a narration of my encounter in a vision with the Lord in which He allowed me to see the things that had rivaled His Lordship in my life.

### Vision of Things That Rivaled God in My Life:
*On this day, I was at one of Pastor Chris's outdoor crusades after I came out of the psychiatric hospital. Praise and Worship was going on and I was all caught up in the Praise and Worship when the Lord opened up heaven to me and said, **"Come up higher."** I saw Him before He spoke to me so in response, I decided to seriously focus on Him but as I tried to rise up higher in the realm of the spirit, I began*

*to see most of my earthly possessions such as my car, my apartment, my clothes, my shoes, my bank accounts, my friends, my job, etc., also demanding that I pay attention to them. Every single one of them had a voice and they were all yelling and demanding my attention.*

*To make matters worse, they also had their strings attached to me so that as I was trying to rise up in the spirit, they were each pulling on the strings in their attempts to pull me back down so that I can pay attention to them! I was shocked and I began the struggle to free myself from them. As I was struggling to get free, I could see the Lord cheering for me to keep pushing them away as He continued to say, "Higher, higher, and higher." I finally got free of them all and was now before Him and He said to me, "By My faith you are healed." This was how the Lord healed and delivered me from the mind vexing spirits that were unleashed against my mind.*

He spoke to me in a most profound way and I learned from this experience that everything that you own has a string and that they talk and vie for your attention as you try to rise up in your spirit to know God deeper. It took a lot of effort for me to let go of all the things that had their strings attached to me and I knew then that it was only by the grace of the Lord that I was able to get free of them. **God wants to give you good things but He does not want those things to own you because you belong to Him.**

For example, there are some Christians that will tell you that their schedules, their family obligations and their jobs or some other "important" activities do not permit them to have a time of devotion with the Lord. A lot of Christians have told me that the only time they have to spend with the Lord is when they are in their cars and on their way to work! This is unacceptable to God because He wants more of you than that.

Also, God is no respecter of persons; therefore, He will work with you so that you too can get rid of everything that is keeping you from rising up to Him. When things rival God in your life, you will not have a successful Christian walk and we can clearly see it in the Lord's Sermon about the Parable of the Sower:

> "**He also that received seed among the thorns** is he that **heareth the word**; and **the care of this world** (*things that vie for your attention*), and **the deceitfulness of riches**, choke the word, and he becometh unfruitful" (Matthew 13:22).

We must know God as the only Supreme Being that can come into our lives to remove the things that rival Him because He is jealous over us. This is critical because some people only see Him as some sort of Santa Clause that they only petition for their needs. You must desire to know Him more than that.

## Knowing God as the Merciful and Gracious One

Yes, God is merciful and God is gracious. He said to Moses in **Exodus 34:6-8** that He is the LORD GOD who is "**Keeping mercy for thousands.**" What this tells us is that God's mercy made Him to send His only begotten Son to save us. After we become born again, we are to be comforted and we are to rest in the hope that whenever we slip and sin, if we repent and purpose not to commit the sin again, God is merciful and that He is gracious enough to forgive and cleanse us of the sin. His mercy and His grace make Him to not hold our sins against us but to work with us until we develop godly character. He has never said to anyone, "I cannot forgive you because my grace and mercy cannot bear the weight of your numerous sins." Even when we messed up the second time, third time, a hundred times, He is willing to work with us until we get it right.

Remember when Peter asked the Lord Jesus how many times he was supposed to forgive his brother who sins against him? He wanted to know if forgiving his brother seven times for the same offence was enough and the Lord said not seven times but seventy times seven times!:

> "Then came Peter to him, and said, Lord, **how oft shall my brother sin against me, and I forgive him? till seven times?** 22 Jesus saith unto him, **I say not unto thee, Until seven times: but, until seventy times seven**" (Matthew 18:21-22).

God's well of mercy and grace is very deep and He wants us all to draw from it on a daily basis so that we can in turn show mercy and grace to those who offend us. How many of us really press in to know that He is truly merciful so that when we are supposed to let those who offend us off the hook, we can do it because of His grace upon our lives?

Also, He wants us to let ourselves off the hook and not beat ourselves down to death for something that we have done and repented of before Him. I have seen many Christians who cannot let go of some sin that they committed against God and repented of. Years later, they are still condemning themselves and cannot rest in the truth that when they repented, God forgave them. The reason for this is because they have a limited knowledge of God's mercy and grace. We must never forget that He is truly merciful and that He is truly gracious. We should always remind ourselves that He genuinely keeps mercy for thousands and that when we sin; He is going to forgive us our sins, our transgressions and our iniquities if we repent.

## Knowing God as the Longsuffering One

One of the attributes of God is that He is longsuffering; meaning that He has an unbelievable length of patience. He can wait for many years on something or for His purposes to come to pass. A good example is His dealing with the children of Israel in the wilderness. Although God showed them many miracles, they still did not believe Him and they murmured

Dr. Mary J. Ogenaarekhua

against Him and against His representative Moses. Therefore, God swore in His anger that they will not go into the Promised Land and He was willing to let them wander in the wilderness for 40 years until they all (except for Joshua and Caleb) died so that He could work with their children:

> "For **the children of Israel walked forty years in the wilderness, till all the people that were men of war, which came out of Egypt, were consumed,** because they obeyed not the voice of the LORD: unto whom the LORD sware that he would not shew them the land, which the LORD sware unto their fathers that he would give us, a land that floweth with milk and honey. 7 **And their children, whom he raised up in their stead, them Joshua circumcised**: for they were uncircumcised, because they had not circumcised them by the way" **(Joshua 5:6-7).**

As we saw before, another way of saying that God is long suffering is found in **1 Corinthians 13:4-8.** The analysis of it helped us to see God's longsuffering nature. Do you remember the previous discussion on **1 John 4:8** which states that **God is love**? Well, it too bears repeating again here. Since **love is the person of God** and charity is another word for love, what **1 Corinthians 13:4-8** is doing is outlining for us the qualities or the characteristic of God as love. Part of His love nature is having a lot of patience.

Therefore, God has a lot of patience and He endures the foolishness that we exhibit before Him on a daily basis for a long time. Also, as a result of the finished works of Christ, He puts up with a lot of nonsense from us but He hopes and believes for the best in us and about us. Here is **1 Corinthians 13:4-8** again:

> "Charity *(love)* **suffereth long,** and is **kind**; charity **envieth not**; charity **vaunteth not itself,**

is **not puffed up,** 5 **Doth not behave itself unseemly, seeketh not her own,** is **not easily provoked, thinketh no evil;** 6 **Rejoiceth not in iniquity,** but **rejoiceth in the truth;** 7 **Beareth all things, believeth all things, hopeth all things, endureth all things.** 8 Charity **never faileth..."**

No one can match God's level of patience and endurance as He lovingly woos us daily and as He pleads with us to choose righteousness and forsake evil. He has patiently endured man's inhumanity to man knowing that His appointed day for man to give account to Him will come. Meanwhile, He is determined to get "godly seed" for Himself in Christ; even if it means enduring the cruelest things that people do to one another on earth without pouring out His instant judgments.

Talking about God's longsuffering nature, I remember some years ago when I was in a conversation with Him and my question to Him was, **"Lord, how could you watch the conditions of black people as slaves in different part of the world and the Nazi's atrocious acts against the Jews and other ethnic groups that took place in Germany during the holocaust as well as some of the most outrageous atrocities that have taken place in the world and not pour out your judgment?"** He took a deep breath and then said to me, **"But, I saw you."** I asked what He meant by that and **He informed me that if He had brought His judgment against the world the way that we sometimes want Him to, I and all those in the world today; especially Christians would not have been born!**

**Everyone alive today is partaking of the longsuffering nature of God.** As a result of His longsuffering nature, God has millions and millions of people in the world today that are the "the seed of Abraham" in Christ Jesus! **In essence, He saw His future Church and as a result, chose to endure some of the most horrible sights of wickedness on earth**

**while refraining Himself from pouring out judgments.** For example, He endured the sight of His only begotten Son Jesus Christ on the way to man's wickedly designed Cross but He had to refrain Himself from intervening because He wanted to have many more sons and daughters in Christ.

If you are ever blessed or privileged to get a heavenly glimpse of God the Father watching His Son as He staggered towards Calvary or Golgotha for crucifixion, you will get a first hand picture of God's longsuffering and at the same time see the level of His indescribable love for humanity. It was an amazing sight to watch Him as He looked in the most sober and refrained manner at His Son as He took every staggering step and eventually got to the place where He would hang for hours before dying. When I saw the extent of His longsuffering and His restraint as He watched His Son, I was beyond **shocked** and I understood that He alone could exercise such restraint. The scene was so intense that **He** could not look upon His Son on that Cross because He cannot look upon sin. In other words, as the Lord Jesus became our sin on the cross, God the Father had to separate Himself from "the sin" that the Lord Jesus had become and the Lord had to endure all the sufferings on the cross as a man (human being) for our sake. He is awesome:

> **"For he hath made him to be sin for us, who knew no sin; that we might be made the righteousness of God in him"** (2 Corinthians 5:21).

**On the other hand, God's longsuffering and patience can cover several generations.** This is where we really have to be careful about the longsuffering nature of God. For example, He can give you a prophetic word or a vision about what He is going to do for you but if you fail to meet His criteria for manifesting that Word or vision in your life, He will wait for your offspring. If your offspring grow up and they too live their lives for themselves and also fail to meet His criteria, He will wait for the next generation and so on.

Therefore, there are many people that have lived and died without ever coming into what God promised them because they do not know this aspect of Him. He has been known to wait for 14 generations before bringing to pass some of the things written in scriptures because He does not change His righteous requirements for anyone. Those who do not know the nature of His longsuffering can walk through life beholding their blessings from afar off and never able to apprehend them because they fail to meet His righteous requirements. God can wait for thousands of generations if need be.

Understanding this side of God helps us to press in to know Him deeper so that we can receive all the blessings that the generations before us could not apprehend. I remember thanking God for His blessing upon my life one day and He said to me, **"You did not ask Me for this. Your father asked Me for this but he could not walk in what he asked for because he did not know spiritual warfare. This is why I raised you up to know spiritual warfare so that you can walk in what he asked for."** He also informed me that my father knew in his spirit that he could not walk in what he asked for so he requested that God let him wait (live) until at least one of his children came into the kingdom of God before he passed away.

Before He told me this, I did not understand why my dad died within two years of my being born again. You see, my father was born into a Muslim family but before the age of 16, he became a Christian and his father promptly disowned him. But, my father read the biblical account of the life of King Solomon and was greatly fascinated by it and he took on the name Solomon. According to the Lord, my father's desire was to be like Solomon but he lived and died without accomplishing this desire.

What the Lord was saying to me in this conversation was that my father asked Him for the blessing of Solomon and He granted my father's request but my father never walked in it in his lifetime. Therefore, the Lord wanted me to know what was already in my spiritual account so that I can apprehend it and walk in it in my life time. Otherwise, He can wait for the next generation.

Yes, God is longsuffering and not knowing Him as such is dangerous for us Christians. Many people are sitting on generational blessings and they do not even know it because they have not yet realized that God's longsuffering will make Him to patiently wait for their generation to expire to make room for the next generation.

## Knowing God as the One Who is Abundant in Goodness

It is true that God is abundant in goodness and you have to know Him on this level also. In other words, you must know that goodness is one of the things that flow from Him; it oozes out of Him like honey. God lays up His goodness for all those who put their trust in Him and that live in reverential fear of Him. **Psalms 31:19** says the following:

> **"Oh how great is thy goodness, which thou hast laid up for them that fear thee; which thou hast wrought for them that trust in thee before the sons of men!"**

Those who do not walk in the fear of the Lord by avoiding evil and living righteously cannot partake of the abundant goodness of God. It is God's goodness that makes Him to pardon our transgression and sin; it makes Him to forgive us of our wrong doings:

> "Remember not the sins of my youth, nor my transgressions: **according to thy mercy**

**remember thou me for thy goodness' sake, O LORD"** (Psalms 25:7).

Every day that we wake up is a testimony of God's goodness because He does not deal with us according to what we deserve but according to His goodness; He has mercy upon us daily. Therefore, for someone not to get to know Him as the one who gives us our daily bread, divine health, and satisfies our daily needs because of His goodness is to live short of the goodness of God.

Those who cannot recognize God's goodness in their daily lives murmur and complain against Him and as such take themselves out of the place of blessing because God loves a grateful heart. One of the things that scriptures tell us in **Ephesians 3:20** is that God's goodness makes Him to do exceeding and abundantly above what we ask Him:

> "Now unto **him that is able to do exceeding abundantly above all that we ask or think,** according to the power that worketh in us..."

Get to know God as one who is abundant in goodness and quit murmuring and complaining when things do not go the way you want. Always remember that it is the goodness of God that makes Him give you the very breath that you breathe every day. You did not and cannot pay for it and the day your breath is taken away, you are out of here.

## Knowing God as the One Who is Abundant in Truth

Also, we must know God as the one that is full of Truth. Many will wonder what this means. The Lord Jesus told us in **John 17:17** that **God's Word is Truth:**

> **"Sanctify them through thy truth: <u>thy word is truth</u>."**

**Since the Word of God is the truth that sets every man and woman free on planet earth according to the Word of God in John 8:32,** *("and ye shall know the truth, and the truth shall make you free"),* **it is in our best interest to know God by His Word.** The children of Israel saw more miracles than any human being who is alive today, **yet they could not walk successfully with God because they did not know Him by His Word.**

You can witness a lot of miracles on a constant basis but without the Word of God to ground you in what you are seeing and experiencing, it is only a matter of time before the devil comes in to try to pervert your perception or make your mind dull concerning them. The miracles, signs and wonders that you witnessed can quickly become some feel good experience and their memory can quickly fade into the past. As a result, you can become like the children of Israel in the wilderness who witnessed great miracles but murmured and judged God for whatever they wanted that He did not manifest for them instantly.

On His part, God was determined to make sure that the children of Israel knew that His Word was more important to them than the very food that they eat every day. As a result, He led them through a terrible wilderness full of all types of hardships for that reason:

> **"And thou shalt remember all the way which the LORD thy God led thee these forty years in the wilderness, to humble thee, and to prove thee, to know what was in thine heart, <u>whether thou wouldest keep his commandments, or no</u>** *(His Word)***.** 3 And he humbled thee, and suffered thee to hunger, and fed thee with manna, which thou knewest not, neither did thy fathers know; **that he might make thee know that <u>man doth not live by bread only, but by every word that</u>**

**proceedeth out of the mouth of the LORD doth man live**" (Deuteronomy 8:2-3).

Today, God is doing the same thing with us who come to Him in Christ because He wants us to learn the same lesson. **Many Christians go to church but they do not spend time with God and His Word. Therefore, they are not grounded in God's Word that reveals God's ways, His nature and His expectations to them.** If like the children of Israel you fail or are unwilling to learn the importance or the value of God's Word in your life, He will allow your life to be "a terrible wilderness." God can wait until you realize the importance of His Word in your life and until you give it the preeminence that it deserves. If like the children of Israel you refuse to learn this valuable lesson, He will wait for your next generation.

**Those who only seek Him for material things can die in their needs and never receive what they petitioned Him for because His priority is for all of us to first know Him by His Word then He will bless us with material things.** This is why the Lord Jesus told us in **Matthew 6:33** to seek first the kingdom of God and His righteousness and the things that we need will then be given to us:

> "**But <u>seek ye first the kingdom of God</u>, and his righteousness; and <u>all these things shall be added unto you</u>.**"

According to the Lord, the heathen only seek God for what they can get out of Him and they do not receive these things from Him but the Lord Jesus told us not to be like them. Remember what God said to King Solomon when Solomon asked Him for wisdom and knowledge in **2 Chronicles 1:10-12**?:

> "**Give me now wisdom and knowledge,** that I may go out and come in before this people: for who can judge this thy people, that is so great? *11* **And God said to Solomon,** Because

this was in thine heart, and thou hast **not asked riches, wealth, or honour, nor the life of thine enemies, neither yet hast asked long life; but hast asked wisdom and knowledge for thyself, that thou mayest judge my people, over whom I have made thee king**: *12* Wisdom and knowledge is granted unto thee; **and I will give thee riches, and wealth, and honour, such as none of the kings have had that have been before thee, neither shall there any after thee have the like."**

This is a powerful key for all those who want God to bless them materially. First, find out His priority and He will give you what you need. Below is an account of my personal vision of how God has placed a great priority in our knowing His Word.

### A Vision of God's Order of Priority
### Concerning My Petitions

*I was praying and making petitions to God about the many "urgent" needs in my life and one day, God the Father showed up in a vision in my apartment. In this vision, I was with Him in His classroom in heaven and He was dressed like a college professor. With a smile, He pointed His finger to the board on His classroom wall. He then informed me that on the board were all the prayers and petitions that I have prayed and all the prayers and petitions that I will ever pray in my lifetime. He then allowed me to see that He had personally arranged my prayers and petitions in His order of priority.*

*I saw that number one was **knowledge**, followed by **wisdom, understanding**, and so on. My personal needs did not even make the top 20 but they were all there and the board was full with just my prayers and petitions. Without saying a word to me, He picked up His classroom chalk* *and went to the board and while there, **He checked off knowledge**. He then turned to me and said, **"What you need is knowledge because you are yet too ignorant for all these other things that you are asking for"** as He pointed to the rest of the list. Without saying another word, the vision was over.*

From this vision, I personally saw the great importance that He had placed on our knowing His Word. God is abundant in goodness and mercy and He will do for you exceedingly and abundantly above what you asked Him for but you must purpose in your heart to first know Him by His Word. His Word is the only truth that there is because all the other doctrines and their voices on earth are nothing but lies.

## Knowing God as the One Who Forgives

Our God is a forgiving God and He actually delights in forgiving us because He loves us and does not want us to perish. The Bible says in **Romans 3:23** that, **"All have sinned and come short of the glory of God."** Therefore, forgiving sins is part of God's divine nature. He is Love and He loves to forgive. He sent His only begotten Son into the world to suffer, be humiliated and die a painful cruel death on the Cross so that He can forgive us our sins by washing us in His Son's blood!:

> **"In whom we have <u>redemption through his blood, the forgiveness of sins</u>, according to the riches of his grace"** (Ephesians 1:7).

It is the power of God's forgiveness that reunited us to Him by His Son and it is the power of His forgiveness that keeps us all throughout our Christian walk. My question is; how many of us truly know the power of God's forgiveness enough to not beat down ourselves when we sin? He promised to forgive us when we repent but many people do not have a revelation of

His forgiving power and as a result, they cannot ease up on themselves when they sin or mess up and they have genuinely asked God for forgiveness. The Bible tells **in 1 John 1:9** that:

> **"If we confess our sins, He is faithful and just to forgive us our sins, and to cleanse us from all unrighteousness."**

We must have a revelation of this so that we do not continue to hold onto something that we did and repented of years ago. When God forgives, He also forgets and He wants us to do the same with ourselves and with others.

## Knowing God as the One Who By No Means Clears the Guilty

One of the scary sides of God is that He has a very good memory and He sees everything and He does not accept excuses from those who sin and do not repent. Therefore, when a person sins and tries to cover it up or begins to make excuses, the sin remains and one day, God judges or holds the person accountable for what he or she has done. There are times that He would allow the person to be made a public spectacle by the unbelievers as the person's sins are broadcasted all over the person's neighborhood or the media.

The Bible says that God **"will by no means clear the guilty"** (Exodus 34:7). Without repentance, God does not remit sins. It does not matter how close you are to Him or how long you have been walking with Him; when you sin, you must repent or He will visit you with judgment as the Righteous Judge that He is. If you cover up your sin or refuse to repent of your sin because you think you have a special place with God, He will let you see a side of Him that is scary. Therefore, you cannot say to yourself, "Wait a minute; I have gone to a level in God that He can cut me some slack because I am extra special to Him."

**If you deceive yourself with such a lofty idea, He will visit you with His judgment and sometimes, He might send an adversary against you that will make sure that your sins are made public because some of the consequences of sin are <u>shame</u> and <u>humiliation</u>. He will let you suffer both as a lesson to others who are covering their sins in secret places and as a just punishment for you.**

Therefore, it is beneficial to know Him as the God who will by no means clear the guilty. This is why no matter how great you are in your ministry; you cannot cut yourself any slack when it comes to sin and God's requirements for righteousness. If you do, it means that you do not know Him as **the God who will by no means excuse the guilty**. He will not clear you by saying, "Bless your heart, I just saw you do that and I also saw your excuse for not repenting and I understand." As you saw in the book of Genesis, an excuse did not work when Adam used one with God in **Genesis 3:12:**

> **"And the man said, the woman whom thou gavest to be with me, she gave me of the tree, and I did eat."**

Adam blamed Eve rather than repent for eating the fruit that God personally told him not to eat. Again, the Bible says that without repentance, there is no remission of sin. There has to be repentance because if no one will repent, everyone suffers. This is who God is; He will by no means acquit the guilty. He will not clear you just because you come to Him every day and worship Him while you have a secret sin hidden. If you do not repent of the sin, you can be having conversations with Him in other areas of your life but remember how He dealt with King David. King David's situation with Bathsheba is a very good example of God's delayed judgment for a season in one area of a person's life.

King David sinned because he thought that his intimacy with God gave him a special status so that he can take some ungodly liberties for himself even if he has to take another person's life. He began by coveting Bathsheba and sleeping with her but when she got pregnant, his special status' view of himself surfaced. As the King, he was supposed to administer the law of God concerning adultery but instead of submitting Bathsheba and himself to the High Priest for judgment, he devised an evil way to get out of the situation.

He sent for Bathsheba's husband Uriah from the war front and when he could not get him to go home to his wife so that when Bathsheba's pregnancy began to show everyone would assume that Uriah was the father, he had him killed. David immediately married Bathsheba and they had a son. What is interesting about the ways of God in this story is that David and Bathsheba actually lived together for several months after the death of Bathsheba's husband before she gave birth. The child lived briefly and got sick and David was on his face praying and fasting before God for days until the child died and yet, God said nothing to David.

Meanwhile, before the child's death, David like many people in the church today was going to the temple praising God and singing "shandra" regularly until the day that God sent David His judgment. As I said earlier, God will not forgive anyone who will not repent of his or her sin. This is a vital aspect of God that you need to know so that you do not allow your sins and your iniquities to pile up before Him and not repent. Because He is the God who will by no means clear the guilty, He has a Judgment Day prepared for all who will not repent of their sins. It is our job to repent of them so that He can restore those areas of our lives.

Otherwise, I will say again that just like King David, you can be going to church and singing "Shandra" as well but when you get home the devil will use circumstances and adverse situations to say to you, "You are mine in this area" because God is not your Lord God in this particular area of your life. Since you are not submitted to God in this particular area of your life, the devil will continue to wrestle with you while at the same time you run the risk of incurring God's judgment.

This is why the Lord said in **Matthew 7:22-23** that on Judgment Day He is going to reject some people who did what was right in their own eyes instead of doing what God wanted them to do. Iniquity (the tendency to do your own thing) is a sin before God and we need to repent of it when we realize it. All those who lived their lives in iniquity will be rejected by the Lord on Judgment Day:

> **"Many will say to me in that day, Lord, Lord, have we not prophesied in thy name? and in thy name have cast out devils? and in thy name done many wonderful works?** And then will I profess unto them, **I never knew you: depart from me, ye that work <u>iniquity</u>."**

Moses is a very good example of one who was not allowed to go into God's promise land although he walked so very closely with God. This is the same Moses that used to stand before God and say to God, "Please do not destroy this people." In an instant, God judged him and his brother Aaron the High Priest and God told Moses to go and look at the Promised Land; I mean He told Moses to go and take a good look at it because He will not allow him to step one foot into it. To make matters worse, He told Moses to go to a mountain side and die there because of his disobedience to Him. Remember that this is the same Moses who was walking so closely with God. This is our God in action letting Moses know the importance of obedience to His Word.

In the final analysis, it all came down to obeying God's instructions. The first time the children of Israel cried because of lack of water, God told Moses **to strike the Rock** and that water will come out. Moses struck the Rock and water came out. Again, the children of Israel cried for lack of water and this time around, God told Moses to **speak to the Rock** but rather than speaking to the Rock, <u>Moses' sin was that he struck the Rock the second time instead of speaking to it</u> as God commanded him. His disobedience of God's instruction to speak to the Rock cost him the Promised Land.

To an average person, the judgment that Moses received might seem drastic but when God gives you a spiritual revelation of the significance of speaking to the Rock rather than striking the Rock a second time, then you will know why God was angry and why He judged Moses so harshly. **The Bible tells us that the Rock is Christ!** The Rock represented Christ the ROCK OF OUR SALVATION! As our Messiah, Christ can only be struck once and it was done on the Cross.

Christ was crucified once and for all, now we are to speak to Him as our ROCK for whatsoever we need. He cannot be crucified a second time. Therefore, what seemed like a small oversight from our human perspective concerning Moses' action is really a colossal act of transgression from God's perspective. The finished works of Christ were too great to be undone or nullified by an act of disobedience by Moses.

## Knowing God as the One Who Visits Iniquities upon Generations

As a Righteous Judge, God will visit the iniquity of the fathers and the mothers upon their future generations. You must know this aspect of His nature so that you can put iniquity out of your life. If not, then, know that your future generations will also pay for the iniquities that you committed against God and did not repent of; they will continue to pay even up to the third and fourth generations! Yes, God will visit your iniquities upon your children and your children's children.

Again, there is a drastic side of God that we must all know so that we can walk in fear of Him. Just think about it, He will one day send some people to hell; a very horrible place! This is why we are told in **Galatians 6:7** that we should not be deceived because God's judgments are righteous and appropriate:

> **"Be not deceived; God is not mocked: for whatso-ever a man soweth, that shall he also reap."**

That is why we talk about breaking generational curses because as the one who visits iniquities on future generations, God is to be feared. I know that some people do not believe that they should walk in the fear of God but I tell you this; the more you know Him, the more you want to fear Him because of His awesome power and His righteous standards. He will by no means acquit the guilty so it is up to us to repent when we see the ungodly things that have been done in our family by the previous generations.

While talking to Abraham, God told him that He will not bring His judgment against the Amorites in Abraham's days because their cup of iniquity was not yet full. In other words, He told Abraham that He will not dispossess the Amorites from their land and give the land to Abraham and his seed just yet because He is looking at the iniquity cup of the Amorites and it is not yet full.

Therefore, God waited four hundred years between Abraham and the time of Moses to judge the Amorites. When their cup was filled up, then He brought forth His judgment against them just as He did in Sodom and Gomorrah:

> "But in the fourth generation they shall come hither again: **for the <u>iniquity of the Amorites is not yet full</u>**" (Genesis 15:16).

I believe that just as the Amorites **"cup of iniquity"** was filling up with sins before God generations after generations, every nation and every family have **"a cup of iniquity"** before God also. As God watches this cup fill up with sins without repentance by a nation, a family or a person in each generation, eventually God brings forth His Judgment. When this happens, you can say that the nation, the family or the person's sin has found them out according to **Numbers 32:23**:

> "But if ye will not do so, behold, ye have sinned against the LORD: **and be sure your sin will find you out.**"

## *Chapter 5*
## Knowing God by Names
## that Reveal His Functions

### Knowing God as a Consuming Fire

God sent prophets after prophets into the earth and finally, He sent His Son; our Lord Jesus Christ to inform us to turn away from iniquity and unto Him. Today, He uses His Church to deliver the message of salvation and all those who refuse to take heed of His Word are living a very dangerous life because **God is a consuming fire.** He will consume all who die in their sins according to **Hebrews 12:25-29:**

> **"See that ye refuse not him that speaketh. For if they escaped not who refused him that spake on earth, much more shall not we escape, if we turn away from him that speaketh from heaven:** *26* Whose voice then shook the earth: but now he hath promised , saying, Yet once more I shake not the earth only, but also heaven. *27* And this word, Yet once more, signifieth the removing of those things that are shaken, as of things that are made, that those things which cannot be shaken may remain. *28* Wherefore we receiving a kingdom which cannot be moved, **let us have grace, whereby we may serve God acceptably with reverence and godly fear:** *29* For our God is a consuming fire."

As I showed you earlier, God promised in **Revelation 20:12-15** that as the Landlord of the earth, He is going to hold everyone accountable for what they did while they were living on His earth. Yes, He is going to judge everyone's works. Therefore, living by God's Word is the only way that anyone can truly know what God expects us all to do while living on His earth. As a result, those who only knew Him as the owner of the earth but wanted nothing further to do with Him while they were alive are going to come short of His expectations. When they are judged, they are going to be found wanting:

> **"And I saw the dead, small and great, stand before God; and the books were opened: and another book was opened, which is the book of life: and the dead were judged out of those things which were written in the books,** <u>according to their works</u>. *13* And the sea gave up the dead which were in it; and death and hell delivered up the dead which were in them: and they were judged every man <u>according to their works</u>. *14* And death and hell were **cast into the lake of fire**. This is the second death. *15* **And whosoever was not found written in the book of life was <u>cast into the lake of fire</u>."**

Also, God promised in **Malachi 4:1** to judge those who rejected Him in their lifetime with fire. He promised to bring fire upon the earth to burn ungodly men and women with it:

> **"For, behold, the day cometh, that shall burn as an oven; and all the proud, yea, and all that do wickedly, shall be stubble: and the day that cometh shall burn them up, saith the LORD of hosts, that it shall leave them neither root nor branch."**

Again, He said in **Revelation 16:8** that He will send His angel to scorch the ungodly with fire:

> **"And the fourth angel poured out his vial upon the sun; and power was given unto him to <u>scorch men with fire</u>."**

There are those on earth today who insist on casting out God from their lives as they believe and promote doctrines which state that there was never a God, that God is dead or that God does not exist. They are not only unbelieving but they turn those who would believe in God away with their evil doctrines. According to God, they will have their part in the lake of fire:

> "But **the fearful,** and **unbelieving,** and **the abominable,** and **murderers,** and **whoremongers,** and **sorcerers,** and **idolaters,** and **all liars,** shall have their part in the lake which burneth with fire and brimstone: **which is the second death**" (Revelation 21:8).

As we saw in a previous chapter, being **Lord** of the earth means that God owns everything. Many of us that have had landlords know what a Lord is. It is someone who is the legal owner of where you dwell. In other words, it is the person or persons that you are renting your dwelling place from. It is the same thing with God when it comes to the earth and all those that dwell in it.

Again, there are some people who are here on earth today who only know God as their landlord because the earth belongs to Him. They want nothing to do with Him and they do not want to put their trust in Him or have Him give them instructions on how to live on His earth. From the scriptures that I showed you, you can clearly see what is going to happen to these types of people who do not know God beyond His being their Landlord.

This is why He has been telling everyone in the whole world to change from the place of unbelief and to place their faith in His Son because **it is a spiritual suicide for a person not to know God beyond just occupying His land on earth.** Everyone must know Him and subject him or herself to His rules and regulations in the Bible or they will not be able to escape the condemnation that awaits them on Judgment Day. To the wicked, our God is a consuming fire. As I have said repeatedly, our God is very, very patient **but**

**He can also erupt like a volcano**. God's judgment consumes just like fire; it consumes all sins, iniquities, transgressions **and finally all those who will not submit to His kingdom rule and authority**.

## Knowing God as the I AM

As I promised in Chapter 2, we are now going to take a look at how God functions as the **I AM THAT I AM.** We have already seen that He told Moses that His name is the **I AM THAT I AM.** Therefore, you need to know Him as such so that as the **I AM**, He can show up and deliver you or do whatever you need Him to at any given time. You might be in need of healing, you might be in need of spiritual deliverance from demonic oppression, or you might be in need of restoration of a relationship and His promise to you is, "**I AM** more than able to do all of them and more."

What He was telling us when He said that His name is the **I AM,** is that whatever we need for Him to be in our lives, "**I AM** equal to the task." Meaning, **I Am** the one for you to call upon when you need help on earth and I can handle any situation that life might throw at you –**Exodus 3:13-14:**

> "And Moses said unto God, Behold, when I come unto the children of Israel, and shall say unto them, The God of your fathers hath sent me unto you; **and they shall say to me, What is his name? what shall I say unto them?** *14* And God said unto Moses, **I AM THAT I AM: and he said, Thus shalt thou say unto the children of Israel, <u>I AM hath sent me unto you</u>**."

Four hundred years before the **I AM** delivered the children of Israel from bondage in Egypt, He told Abraham about it when He was talking to Abraham in the book of Genesis. He told Abraham that his descendants were going to be enslaved in a foreign land for four hundred years and that at the end of those four hundred years, He will bring them out. God was faithful to keep His Word. He raised up a deliverer for them in the person of Moses when the four hundred years were completed as we see in **Exodus 3:8:**

> "And **I AM come down to deliver them out of the hand of the Egyptians**, and to bring them up out of that land unto a good land and a large, unto a land flowing with milk and honey; unto the place of the Canaanites, and the Hittites, and the Amorites, and the Perizzites, and the Hivites, and the Jebusites."

The **I AM** keeps His promises no matter what. The children of Israel that were under Moses were not the generation that He directly made the promise of deliverance to but to Abraham their forefather. Due to His faithfulness, He remembered His promise to His friend Abraham and He delivered on that promise. **We must know this about Him so that we can rest in the hope that He is faithful to keep His promises to us also.** When He makes you a promise, He is going to remember it whether or not you remember it and He is going to do what He promised.

My personal experience with Him about how faithfully He remembers His promises even when we forget was with the promise that He made to me when I took a fatal fall and died. During my encounter with Him on the other side and before He sent me back the next day, He said to me, **"Go and get yourself baptized and I will show you things."** This happened when I was 9 years old. I was just learning the English language so I had no idea what the word "baptize" meant. Also, I was living with my grandparents who were Muslims and I did not even know that "baptize" was a Christian term. Although I later found out what baptism was as I attended a Roman Catholic School, yet, I did not remember His promise. Over the years, I forgot all together His promise that He will **show me things**.

Quite frankly, I do not think that I gave it a second thought because I was not yet familiar with Christianity to know that God speaks and shows things to His children. It was many years later that I became born again. Not long after my new birth experience, He came on the scene of my life to begin "showing me things." He actually told me that I forgot the promise but that He remembered it. True to His Word, one of my primary Anointings is the Anointing of discerning what is going on in the realm of the spirit and I teach people how to also discern what goes on in the realm of the spirit.

Not only does He remember His promises but as the **I AM THAT I AM**, God can be whatever is good and godly that we want Him to be for us. Therefore, you need to take the time to study what it means for God to be the **I AM**. One of the reasons for knowing Him by this functioning name is because it is a vital aspect of who He is and in His dealings with us on earth; it encompasses everything that we will ever need from Him. For example, when you see an accident about to happen, call on His name because He is right there for you. When you call on the **I AM** to be the shield between you and the oncoming car ahead of you in the name of the Lord Jesus, He will do it. The Lord Jesus told us that He is the **I AM**; meaning that He was "before Abraham" and that **He is God –John 8:58-59**:

> "Jesus said unto them, **Verily, verily, I say unto you, Before Abraham was, I am**. *59* Then took they up stones to cast at him: but Jesus hid himself, and went out of the temple, going through the midst of them, and so passed by."

He alone can keep us out of danger and from all the wickedness that the devil plans against us. Again, it is the reason He said in **Romans 10:13** that:

**"...Whosoever shall call upon the name of the Lord shall be saved."**

He told me once that a lot of times when negative or evil things are happening to people, they forget to call upon His name. Some people do not even know how to call on Him because they are not used to calling on Him while some people do not believe in calling on Him:

**"How then shall they call on him in whom they have not believed?..."** (Romans 10:14).

Some other people call on the names of their mother, their father, their spouse or their child when something evil is about to happen. Not very many people remember to call on the name of the Lord but those who remember and call on Him are always saved. Today, we call upon the name of His Son in whom He has placed our salvation. Sometimes, the body might be destroyed in the situation or the accident but the soul of that person is saved and the person goes straight on to be with the Lord in heaven. Below is an example:

### The Death of an Only Child

*There was a lady who lost her only daughter in a car accident and the daughter was in her late teens. When I met the lady, it had been three years since the accident but I can tell that this child meant everything to this lady. She still had the daughter's voice on her answering machine, the daughter's pictures in her workspace and she was totally devoid of any joy. Naturally, I felt very, very sorry for her because the child was an only child and she cannot have any more children because of her age. I went to the Lord in prayer because I was curious to find out from Him about this lady's situation. I was told that she was once a very strong Christian and so I wanted the Lord to restore her joy.*

*One of the things that the lady had done was that she stopped going to church and she stopped reading her Bible or having anything to do with God because she felt that He did not protect her only child. She blamed God for what happened. In response to my prayer for the lady, the Lord showed me a vision of the scene of the accident and how the girl had died three years prior. He allowed me to see exactly what happened at the time of the accident.*

*In this vision, the girl was driving back home from school when she had a head on collision with another car. From what I saw, she was a little distracted (looking for something in the glove compartment) and did not see the other car coming straight at her car until it was too late but at the point of impact she cried out, "Jesus" and it was the last thing out of her mouth. The Lord then informed me that because the girl called on Him at the point of the impact, He was right there with her and that she was with Him; she did not perish!*

*In my excitement, I wanted to tell the mother not to cry anymore because her child is with the Lord, but the Lord said No. He told me not to tell her because she had idolized the daughter to the point that she had become a demi-god in her life. According to Him, she needed to come to the realization that no matter what happens in her life, she needs to know that God alone is God and not that child. God as the **I AM** can be anything that she wanted had she gone to Him. He was still waiting for her to come to that revelation.*

God judges any idols that we set up. He will remove an idol in your life even when that idol is your child or your spouse but He will see to it that their souls are saved. Therefore, do not set anyone up as your idol and do not allow anyone to set you up as their idol. If you do, **know that God sets a day aside in which He visits idols to throw them down.**

Finally, we all must strive to know that the **I AM** is our comforter, our righteousness, our redeemer, our avenger, our defender, our provider, our provision, our protector, our deliverer, our healer, our health, our sufficiency, etc. As I said, this aspect of God's name encompasses everything that we will ever need Him to be or need from Him.

## Knowing God as Elohim — the Creator

Another way you need to know the LORD God is as Elohim (the creator). **Elohim** is the plural of **Eloah**. It is the plural form of God that we refer to as **the Godhead** (God the Father, God the Son and God the Holy Ghost). This is where the belief in the Trinity or the Triune God began because they are three persons in one God and we refer to them as the Godhead. This is why when God was talking in **Genesis 1:26** He said:

> **"Let Us make man in our own image and after our likeness..."**

When God uses the words **us** and **our**, your immediate question is, "Who is He talking to and how many of them are there? This is why the Word **Elohim** denotes more than one entity existing as one and we refer to it as the **Godhead.** Although we are talking about three distinct individuals in one, we must know that they are one in unity, will, desire and in all functions. This is the part of God's existence that transcends the finite mind of man and it does not fit into the logical Greek thinking pattern or thoughts that we learned in school.

Although we know them as **God the Father, God the Son** and **God the Holy Ghost**, they are really one. The easiest way to understand this is to know that the Lord Jesus is the Word that came out of God's mouth and the Holy Ghost is God's own spirit. Jesus (God's Word) took on a human form when God spoke His Word into Mary's womb because God functions by using His own Spirit and His own Word. **Because He is God, the three aspects of who He is (Him, His Word and His Spirit) can manifest as three personalities while still remaining as one God.** This is the mystery of the trinity or the Godhead.

As you will read in the next few pages, I have had the privilege of seeing the three of them at the same time and I was amazed at what I saw. They are unified when they speak and when they act; they are not in contradiction to one another because they are one. In **Genesis 3:22,** we see God again using the **plural form of the Godhead (Elohim)** after Adam and Eve rejected Him as their **LORD God** by their submission to the devil's dominion:

> "And the LORD God said, **Behold, the man is become as <u>one of us</u>,** to know good and evil: and now, lest he put forth his hand, and take also of the 'Tree of Life', and eat, and live forever."

God invested Himself in man when He gave man life through His own breath. Therefore, He cares deeply for man and He wants nothing but abundant life, peace, joy, health, etc., for man. His desire was for man to feed from the **"Tree of Life."** It is interesting that Adam and Eve did not gravitate towards the **"Tree of Life"** but towards the **"Tree of the Knowledge of good and evil."** If they had eaten of the "Tree of Life" first, we would have been alive forever in the midst of sins, wickedness, sicknesses and diseases.

This is why God was concerned about man putting forth his hand towards the **"Tree of Life."** If God had allowed man to eat the fruit of the **"Tree of life"** in man's fallen state, we would not have known physical death and physical death would not have had any effect on us but then, man would live in misery forever. God loves man too much to let this happen. **He made man in His own image and having to watch man in a state of misery and wretchedness forever was not something that He wanted us or Himself to endure.** It would have been a problem for Him for all eternity.

Therefore, God the Father, God the Son and God the Holy Spirit **(Elohim)** all agreed that since **man has now experienced a taste of evil,** they did not want man to dwell in the Garden of Eden anymore so that man does not eat from the **"Tree of Life"** and live forever. **In other words, if God does not drive them out of the garden and they eat the fruit from the "Tree of Life," they can keep evil alive forever.** As a result, God drove Adam and his wife out of the Garden of Eden and He set a sword which turns every which way around the **"Tree of Life"** to keep Adam and Eve away from it. **God wanted to be able to get rid of evil (sin) without man attaining to the point where God cannot get rid of evil because evil was now a part of man's eternal nature.**

Another thing was that God did not want man to now live forever and not be on God's side for all eternity. Can you imagine God having to deal with us for all of eternity in our rebellious state? Because God did not want to deal with our rebellious state forever, He put man out of His garden.

### *God as Elohim Continues…*

Again, we see God in **Genesis 11:7** refer to Himself in the plural form **(Elohim)** when He was talking about the rebellious works of Nimrod. As stated in the Bible (Genesis chapters 10 and 11), Nimrod was the great great-grandson of Noah. According to **Flavius Josephus** in his book titled, *Antiquities of the Jews,* Nimrod heard about the flood that took place in the days of his great great-grandfather Noah and he became angry with God because of it. Nimrod was very much anti-God and the following is Josephus' account of Nimrod and his work:

"2. (113) **Now it was Nimrod who excited them to such an affront and contempt of God.** *He was the grandson of Ham, the son of Noah, a bold man, and of great strength of hand. He persuaded them to ascribe it to God, as if it was through his (Nimrod's) means that they were happy, but to believe that it was their own courage which procured that happiness. (114) He also gradually changed the government into tyranny, seeing no other way out of turning men from the fear of God, but to bring them into a constant dependence on his power.*

**He also said he would be avenged in God, if he should have a mind to drown the world again: for he would build a tower too high for the waters to be able to reach: and that he would avenge himself on God for destroying their forefathers.** *3. (115)* <u>**Now the multitude were very ready to follow the determination of Nimrod and to esteem it a piece of cowardice to submit to God;**</u> **and they built a tower, neither sparing any pain, nor being in any degree negligent about the work;** *and, by reason of multitude of hands employed in it, it grew very high, sooner than anyone could expect."*

From the above writing by Josephus, you can see Nimrod's rationale for building the Tower of Babel. Nimrod was ignorant of God's promise to Noah that He would never flood the earth again and he also never bothered to find out the covenant that God made with Noah and all living things that was signified by the Rainbow. As a result, he embarked on a rebellious path taking everyone that was subject to him in his kingdom with him on the same path. His zeal and determination prompted the Godhead **(Elohim)** to get together again in counsel to determine what to do about the rebellion that they saw in Nimrod and his subjects.

**Elohim** (the Godhead) looked at them as they were zealously determined to complete their rebellious tower and **Elohim** said, if left alone, Nimrod and his subjects will actually be able to do whatever they set their hearts on. Therefore, Elohim had to act in **Genesis 11:6-9:**

> "And the LORD said, Behold, the people is one, and they have all one language; and this they begin to do: **and now nothing will be restrained from them, which they have imagined to do**. *7* Go to, **let us go down** *(God speaking as Elohim)*, **and there confound their language, that they may not understand one another's speech.** *8* So the LORD scattered them abroad from thence upon the face of all the earth: <u>and they left off to build the city</u>. *9* Therefore is the name of it called Babel; because the LORD did there confound the language of all the earth: and from thence did the LORD scatter them abroad upon the face of all the earth."

**Elohim** used confusion to destroy Nimrod and his subjects' plans to rebel against Him and to find an escape route from Him. If you think that Nimrod's plans were crazy and absurd, do not because there are many people in the world today that think that they too can devise an escape route from God and His Judgment. They promote pagan religions that rival the belief in the Judeo-Christian God while others promote the idea that God does not exist but what they all fail to realize is that on His appointed day, God will answer them as **Elohim** and He will also confound them, their fancy, their demonic doctrines and their plans.

When the Godhead (Elohim) takes counsel to bring a judgment against a person or a people group, it is a most serious thing because God declared in **Isaiah 45:21-23** that besides Him, there is no God or Savior:

> "...**And there is no God else beside me; a just God and a Saviour; there is none beside me.** 22 **Look unto me, and be ye saved, all the ends of the earth: for I am God, and there is none else.** 23 I have sworn by myself, the word is gone out of my mouth in righteousness, and shall not return, **That unto me every knee shall bow, every tongue shall swear** *(confess or submit)."*

No one will be able to escape the creator on the day that He comes to see about His creation. Therefore, we need to know this aspect of Him so that we can reverence Him accordingly.

**The Lord Jesus really helps us understand God as Elohim** because He talks about Himself, then He talks about the Father, and He talks about the Holy Spirit. Again, **these are the persons that make up the Godhead that we call Elohim.** When He was here on earth, He constantly reminded His listeners that it was not just Him that was performing the miracles, signs and wonders but that it was Him, the Father and the Holy Spirit.

### *My Visions of Elohim: the Godhead*
As far as I am concerned, I am fully persuaded as many other Christians are that the belief in the Godhead is not a figment of the imaginations of Christians. When you become born again and God gives you the gift of seeing into the realm of the spirit, you can actually see God the Father, God the Son, and God the Holy Spirit acting as one God (the Godhead). They are one God in unity and in operation. Below are a couple of accounts of some of my personal encounters with the three persons of the Godhead –**Elohim.**

#### *Vision 1:*
*About seven months after my salvation, I was greatly tormented by the devil and his evil spirits to the point that I ended up in a psychiatric hospital. After my release from*

*a second stay in the hospital, I decided to go to Nigeria to seek deliverance. While I was there, I began to study the Word of God and to learn how to pray using God's Word. I remember being in a church service and the devil began to show me an evil distortion of a person's face, ears and mouth.*

*As I was watching the person's face elongate out of proportion and the ears stretch out to the size of a dinner plate, I began to confess the memory verse (scripture) that I had learned a few days before, "I am not moved by what I see but by the Word of God because it is written, 'We walk by faith and not by sight.'" As I continued to defy what I was seeing and to confess God's Word instead, I began to smell the Anointing (olive) Oil. In my ignorance, I thought someone was using the oil to cook in the nearby house but the Lord wanted me to learn about Him as Elohim and about His Anointing.*

*Therefore, the more I tried to close my nose to the smell of the olive oil, the more He released the smell from on high. I was genuinely shocked that God would use oil in the church. The smell of it was getting too much for me because being that I was from West Africa, I was not used to the smell of olive oil. As I struggled to shield my nose from the smell, the Lord parted heaven for me and I got my first vision of Elohim as they stand in counsel.*

*In this vision, I ran to them in tears crying but when I opened my mouth to launch my complaint about what the devil was doing to me, I heard a voice saying, **"Do not even mention his name for I will show him how much he must suffer for what he has done to my children."** I stood perplexed before them as the words were spoken to me because all three of them **seemed** to be speaking and I could not pin-point which one of them was actually the one speaking. I became determined to discover who was speaking among the three of them.*

*It was one of the most hilarious spiritual experiences that I have had because, God the Father, God the Son and God the Holy Spirit were all trying not to burst into laughter as they watched me seriously determine to find out who was speaking among them by checking out each of their mouths as I was hearing the voice! It was some years later that the Lord reminded me of the encounter and how they thought it so funny that I was determined to solve the mystery of the Godhead.*

Due to the ignorance I displayed in the visions above concerning the Godhead, you can now understand why God had to teach me about who He is and about the Godhead. As a result of the spiritual discernment gifts that He has now given me, I frequently see God the Father and the Lord Jesus in visions and dreams individually and sometimes together. I sometimes see God the Holy Spirit by Himself also, but once I saw God the Father and God the Holy Spirit together in a night vision. Below is the account of my encounter with both God the Father and God the Holy Spirit. Remember that I am only able to see visions by the aid of the Holy Spirit because I am in Christ and Christ is in God and is God's Word. Therefore, all three of the persons of the Godhead are always involved in an activity.

In this vision that I am about to share with you below, God showed me that just like the children of Israel, I was not being a good wife to Him.:

> "Not according to the covenant that I made with their fathers in the day that I took them by the hand to bring them out of the land of Egypt; which my covenant they brake, **although I was an husband unto them, saith the LORD**" (Jeremiah 31:32).

As you have seen in the scripture above, God always regarded Israel as His bride or His wife but they were ungrateful and God hated that. He wanted to correct my ungrateful attitude.

*Vision 2:*

In this vision, the Lord Holy Spirit was acting as the Maitre d' over God's vast mansion and He also was the Bouncer of intruders. I on the other hand, was like a brassy 18 year old that had married a very wealthy older man (God the Father). I drove into this very beautiful beyond description mansion in a sporty convertible car that I had filled up with shopping bags. I had apparently ran out of money while I was shopping and had sent a message to my husband who happens to own this mansion to either send or wire me some money for more shopping and I had not received the money.

Therefore, I was furious at him as I jumped out of the car as soon as I parked it in front of the house and went running up the staircase in this gorgeous mansion screaming, **"Where is he, where is he,"** when the Holy Spirit stepped out from what seemed to have been from nowhere to bounce me out of the house. He did not approve of my rude behavior and my screams so He demanded authoritatively, **"Who is this** (that has the audacity to come in here yelling)? I immediately recognized Him as the Lord Holy Spirit because I had seen Him in other visions before. God the Father was at the top of the staircase in what seemed like an upper room and He replied the Holy Spirit's question by saying, **"She is my wife."** Therefore, the Holy Spirit refrained from His decision to bounce me out of the house as I continued up the staircase in anger.

When I got to God the Father who was my husband in this vision, I attempted to choke Him on the neck because He had not done what I wanted Him to do and when I wanted it done. In His wisdom, He took what seemed like a karate side-step away from me and I missed Him and His neck! With a very broad smile He said to me, **"Ta-da,"** as He moved aside to show me what was behind Him in the upper room. I then saw that behind Him was a table that stretched across the entire length of the *room, covered with white linen and on top of this table was everything that I could ever desire! God the Father as my husband in this vision then proceeded to let me know that while I thought that He was delaying sending me what I wanted, He was actually laying out a table for me with everything that I would ever want on it. What He had prepared for me on that table far exceeded anything that I could have requested from Him.*

*I felt so bad after His words because of the way that I had behaved and for trying to choke Him. I also felt bad about violating the protocol of the house and disrespecting the Holy Spirit. As I was in this emotional state, God the Father and God the Holy Spirit both looked at me as God the Father then declared to me authoritatively saying,* **"until you become the type of wife that I can come home to, I am not letting you near my..."**

After this vision, I knew that if I wanted anything from God, I would have to play by His rules. I cannot get anything out of Him by throwing temper-tantrums, murmuring or complaining about what He has not yet done for me. I knew that I needed a character and an attitude adjustment from Him and I began to cry out for it. I tell you that I had this vision many years ago and even He has told me that He and I have come a long way. I personally know for a fact that God exists in three different personalities as the Father, the Son and the Holy Spirit—**Elohim**. Do not let anyone tell you otherwise.

There are many people today who relate with God the way that I used to relate with Him in the above vision but when you press in deeper and get to know Him, you discover the truth about Him for yourself so that you can walk in a greater trust of Him. I shared these visions above with you to help you understand a little bit more about the working of the Godhead. **I know that we want what we want when we want it, but as you get to know Elohim, you will begin to** rest in His faithfulness and in His mercy. There is nothing that Elohim the creator cannot create for you when you need it; if only you would get to know Him more.

## Knowing God as Our Father

God Himself informed us in **Jeremiah 31:9** that He is a **Father to Israel**: "**...For I am a father to Israel, and Ephraim is my firstborn.**" He wanted to relate to the children of Israel as a father does to his children, but they could not receive Him as such. You can see the cry of His heart in **Malachi 1:6-8** as the children of Israel consistently dishonored Him as a Father:

> "**A son honoureth his father, and a servant his master: if then I be a father, where is mine honour? and if I be a master, where is my fear? saith the LORD of hosts unto you, O priests, that despise my name**. And ye say, Wherein have we despised thy name? 7 Ye offer polluted bread upon mine altar; and ye say, Wherein have we polluted thee? In that ye say, The table of the LORD is contemptible. 8 And if ye offer the blind for sacrifice, is it not evil? and if ye offer the lame and sick, is it not evil? **offer it now unto thy governor; will he be pleased with thee, or accept thy person? saith the LORD of hosts.**"

Today, God is not just a father to Israel but to all who come to Him through His Son Jesus Christ. Therefore, when we bring mediocre offerings to the Lord and we keep the best for ourselves, we dishonor God as our Father. We always have to remember that we give our offerings as unto the Lord. A lot of people spend their money on many worthless things but when they come to church, they drop a miserable $1 in the offering basket for God. I call the things worthless because they cannot bring salvation to a person yet, many people spend their money on them and they do not honor God with their substance. Instead, they dishonor Him by the shabby offerings and gifts that they bring to Him in His house. Unless $1 is truly what you can afford to give, do not dishonor God by not being willing to sacrifice to give Him something worthwhile.

The unfortunate thing is that the same people who give God mediocre offerings are the very people that want God to bless them in their finances, in their relationships and in their many other life endeavors. How can God bless those who dishonor Him? Therefore, we must know God as our Father so that we can give Him the highest honor that He deserves in every area of our lives. Some people are apprehensive about giving in the house of God because of some questionable "ministers." I am not saying that you should give your money to some dubious "minister" but that you should be discerning of where you fellowship or worship.

If the minister is faithfully and sincerely serving God, then, honor God there. Do not throw out the baby with the bath water. Remember that you give your tithes and your offerings to the Lord and not to the minister. God will in turn make the minister to give account of what he or she did with the tithes or offerings collected.

**For us that have been born again,** the Lord Jesus taught us to **relate to God as Our Father** in **Matthew 6:9-13** and when He taught us to pray, He told us to address God as **Our Father**:

> "After this manner therefore pray ye: **Our Father which art in heaven, Hallowed be thy name**. *10* Thy kingdom come. Thy will be done in earth, as it is in heaven. *11* Give us this day our daily bread. *12* And forgive us our debts, as

we forgive our debtors. *13*And lead us not into temptation, but deliver us from evil: For thine is the kingdom, and the power, and the glory, forever. Amen."

And also in **Matthew 6:3-8:**

"But when thou doest alms, let not thy left hand know what thy right hand doeth: *4* That thine alms may be in secret: **and thy Father which seeth in secret himself shall reward thee openly**. *5* And when thou prayest, thou shalt not be as the hypocrites are: for they love to pray standing in the synagogues and in the corners of the streets, that they may be seen of men. Verily I say unto you, **They have their reward.**

*6* **But thou, when thou prayest, enter into thy closet, and when thou hast shut thy door, pray to thy Father which is in secret; and thy Father which seeth in secret shall reward thee openly**... *8* Be not ye therefore like unto them: for **your Father knoweth what things ye have need of, before ye ask him.**"

We are also told in **Matthew 5:9** that as we walk and promote peace among people, we are receiving the blessing of being God's children:

"Blessed are the peacemakers: **for they shall be called the children of God**."

If we are His children, then He is our father. Therefore, one of the ways that we can walk closely with God the Father is to love peace and to advocate it. God loves peace makers and He delights in calling them His children. Making peace brings us closer to Him in our relationship.

In **Romans 8:17,** we learned that we are **Heirs of God and joint-heirs with Christ**. As His children, God the Father has made us co-heirs with His Son Jesus. We need to find out what this means for us in our relationship with Him and His Son today:

> "And **if children, then heirs; <u>heirs of God,</u> <u>and joint-heirs with Christ</u>**..."

Because we are joint-heirs with Christ, He is not ashamed to call us His brethren as stated in **Hebrews 2:17**. This confirms our position with God as His children because even the Lord Jesus deemed it necessary to be made like one of us when He made the decision to come to earth. He chose the form of a man and not the form of an angel. He could have chosen the form of an angel but He did not and He chose to be like us because we are His brothers and sisters:

> "Wherefore **in all things it <u>behoved him</u>** *(necessary)* **to be made like unto his brethren,** that he might be a merciful and faithful high priest in things pertaining to God, to make reconciliation for the sins of the people."

We see from the above scriptures that God delights in relating to us as a Father and that we are to reciprocate by treating Him as such and giving Him the honor that He deserves in our lives on a daily basis. As His children, He wants us to get to know Him very intimately and to be in a daily fellowship with Him. This is where He shares His secrets with His children that have intimacy with Him. Also, as heirs of God and joint heir with Christ, the Lord Jesus bequeathed all that His Father gave Him to us –all things are now ours and as a result, no Christian should suffer lack when he or she submits to God's will.

## Knowing God as Our Teacher

One of the most exciting things about knowing God is to

know Him as our Teacher. I believe that every believer needs to know this side of God because He delights in having a "good student" (one who is hungry for His knowledge) that is willing to learn from Him. I have had Him teach me all night regardless of the fact that I was the only student in His classroom. Yes, God has a classroom that is complete with a board and chalk for writing! Because He is a teacher, He will teach you all things by Himself. Always remember that it is the Holy Spirit that reveals the Father and the Lord Jesus to us; meaning that it is by the help of the Holy Spirit that we see the Father and the Lord Jesus Christ. This is why the Lord said in **John 14:26** that the Holy Spirit will teach us all things:

> "But the Comforter, which is the Holy Ghost, whom the Father will send in my name, **he shall <u>teach you</u> all things, and bring all things to your remembrance**, whatsoever I have said unto you."

Throughout the ages, God the Father has been teaching us first by the Prophets, then by His son and now by His Holy Spirit. When you cry out for knowledge, wisdom and understanding, He will teach you and grant them to you as you walk closely with Him.

## Knowing God as All-Knowing and All-Seeing

Our God is **All-Knowing** (Omniscience); meaning that He knows everything including the secrets things that people hide or do. God knows what is in a person's heart because there is nothing hidden before GOD. What this means for us as we live on His earth is that we must know that there is no escaping God because He is All-Knowing and He is All-Seeing. He cares about His earth and He cares about the people that live on it and He cares about what goes on in it.

The Lord Jesus once told me the following concerning the relationship between Himself and His Father, **"Before I have**

**a thought, my Father is already aware of it!"** There are no secrets between them and because you are a part of them, you should not try to keep secrets from them. The truth is that God sees all things anyway so be real with Him because no one can hide anything from Him. This is why Job declared the following in **Job 26:6-7**:

> **"Hell is naked before him, and destruction hath no covering.** *7* He stretcheth out the north over the empty place, and hangeth the earth upon nothing."

David was also aware of God's Omniscience (All-Knowing), God's Omnipresence (in everywhere), and God's Omnipotence (All-Powerful) as you can see from his cry to God in **Psalms 139:7-12**:

> **"Whither shall I go from thy spirit? or whither shall I flee from thy presence?** *8* If I ascend up into heaven, thou art there: **if I make my bed in hell, behold, <u>thou art there</u>.** *9* If I take the wings of the morning, and dwell in the uttermost parts of the sea; *10* Even there shall **<u>thy hand lead me</u>, and thy right hand shall hold me.** *11* **If I say, Surely the darkness shall cover me; even the night shall be light about me.** *12* **Yea, the <u>darkness hideth not from thee</u>; but the night shineth as the day: <u>the darkness and the light are both alike to thee</u>."**

Also, when you read what the Apostle Paul said in **Hebrews 4:13**, you will again discover that those who walk closely with God are aware that all things are open and naked before Him. There is nothing that anyone can hide in heaven, on earth or in hell from God:

> **"Neither is there any creature that is not manifest in his sight: but all things are naked**

**and opened unto the eyes of him with whom
we have to do."**

Those who do not relate to God as All-Knowing, All-Seeing
and All-Present can ignorantly assume that they can get
away with evil secrets, secret sins, ungodly activities or
some demonically inspired rendez vous. **Those who do
such things are living dangerously because God is not only
All-Knowing; He also has an everlasting memory of un-
repented sins.** Therefore, it is in our best interest to always
remember that He is All-Knowing and All-Seeing so that we
do not think that we can hide something from Him or that we
can get away with a secret sin.

## Knowing God as the Owner of Everything

We must always remember that everything in heaven
and on earth belongs to God and as a result, He makes the
ultimate decision about what goes on here on earth. If you
do not believe this, then read **Job 41:11** to see His very own
Words on the matter:

> "Who hath prevented me, that I should repay
> him? **whatsoever is under the whole heaven
> is mine.**"

Also, **Deuteronomy 10:14** tells us that the whole of heaven,
the earth and everything that is in them belong to the Lord:

> "Behold, **the heaven and the heaven of heavens
> is the LORD'S** thy God, the earth also, with all
> that therein is."

## Knowing God as the One Who Abases the Proud

In your Christian walk, you cannot exalt yourself against
the knowledge of God or above your fellow Christians. If you
do, God knows what to do to get you to the place of humility

and humbleness of heart that He desires for you. You cannot allow even His grace or His Anointing upon your life to make your head swell up with pride because **God always abases the proud and exalts the humble** as stated in **1 Peter 5:5:**

> "...For God <u>resisteth the proud,</u> and <u>giveth grace to the humble.</u>"

Also, in **Ezekiel 21:26** we learned that God delights in seeing the proud person abased and the humble person exalted:

> "Thus saith the Lord GOD; Remove the diadem, and take off the crown: this shall not be the same: **exalt him that is low, and abase him that is hig**h *(proud)*."

**Daniel 4:37** shows how the King Nebuchadnezzar became humble after God publicly abased him and made him live like a wild animal for a while because of his pride:

> "Now I Nebuchadnezzar praise and extol and honour the King of heaven, all whose works are truth, and his ways judgment: **and those that walk in pride he is able to abase**."

One of the questions that God asked Job when He was questioning Job was whether Job can cast his gaze over all the earth and look upon everyone that is proud and abase them all. We see this in **Job 40:8-14:**

> "Wilt thou also disannul my judgment? wilt thou condemn me, that thou mayest be righteous? *9* <u>Hast thou an arm like God? or canst thou thunder with a voice like him?</u> *10* <u>Deck thyself now with majesty and excellency; and array thyself with glory and beauty.</u> *11* **Cast abroad the rage of thy wrath: and behold every one that is proud, and abase him.** *12*

**Look on every one that is proud, and bring him low; and tread down the wicked in their place.** *13* Hide them in the dust together; and bind their faces in secret. *14* Then will I also confess unto thee that thine own right hand can save thee."

Remember that God said the above to Job because Job had foolishly and pridefully accused Him of having been unfair to him when he said the following about God in **Job 9:17-19:**

"For he *(meaning God)* breaketh me with a tempest, and multiplieth my wounds **without cause**. *18* He will not suffer me to take my breath, but filleth me with bitterness. *19* If I speak of strength, lo, he is strong: and if of judgment, who shall set me a time to plead?"

The reality of the matter was that God saw pride in Job and it was the reason why He invited the devil to have a "little go" at Job in order to bring him to the place of humility. The following scriptures in **Job 29:2-25** will give you an insight into what Job thought of himself while he was living in luxury and before his trials began. You can clearly see that he needed to be humbled:

**"Oh that I were as in months past, as in the days when God preserved me**; *3* When his candle shined upon my head, and when by his light I walked through darkness; *4* As I was in the days of my youth, when the secret of God was upon my tabernacle; *5* When the Almighty was yet with me, when my children were about me;

*6* When I washed my steps with butter, and the rock poured me out rivers of oil; *7* **When I went out to the gate through the city, when**

<u>I prepared my seat in the street!</u> *8* **The young men saw me, and hid themselves: and the aged arose, and stood up.** *9* **The princes refrained talking, and laid their hand on their mouth.** *10* **The nobles held their peace, and their tongue cleaved to the roof of their mouth.** *11* **When the ear heard me, then it blessed me; and when the eye saw me, it gave witness to me**:

*12* **Because I delivered the poor that cried, and the fatherless, and him that had none to help him**. *13* <u>The blessing of him that was ready to perish came upon me: and I caused the widow's heart to sing for joy.</u> *14* **I put on righteousness, and it clothed me: <u>my judgment was as a robe and a diadem</u>** *(a crown)*. *15* <u>I was eyes to the blind, and feet was I to the lame.</u>

*16* **I was a father to the poor: and the cause which I knew not I searched out...** *18* **Then I said, I shall die in my nest, and <u>I shall multiply</u> my days as the sand.** *19* **<u>My root was spread out</u> by the waters, and the dew lay all night upon my branch.** *20* <u>My glory was fresh in me, and my bow was renewed in my hand.</u> *21* **<u>Unto me men gave ear, and waited, and kept silence at my counsel</u>.**

*22* **<u>After my words they spake not again; and my speech dropped upon them.</u> 23 And they waited for me as for the rain; and they opened their mouth wide as for the latter rain.** *24* <u>**If I laughed on them, they believed it not; and the light of my countenance they cast not down.**</u> *25* **<u>I chose out their way, and sat chief, and dwelt as a king in the army, as one that comforteth the mourners</u>."**

From these scriptures, you can see the true state of Job's heart and why God had to humble him. What we learn from this is that we should never become prideful or become haughty in the sight of God. No matter what He has given us or how He uses us, we should always remember to remain humble because **God's nature is to abase pride whenever He sees it**. It does not matter how long you have been walking with Him, He hates pride period.

One of the surprising things about getting to know God deeper is how humble He is. Although He is the Almighty and All-Powerful creator of all things; yet, He humbles Himself to relate to His children as a regular father would! I have sometimes asked Him questions thinking that He will say to me "how dare you?" Yet, He would very humbly answer the question or sometimes help me to rephrase the question but He answers the questions to my amazement. Most of the time, while sitting on His heavenly throne, He lets me sit on the ground between His legs and play and it is amazing the interest and delight that He gets just watching me play. At the same time, He does not pretend not to see me when I do something that He disapproves of. Just like any stern father would at such times, He will sharply rebuke me. It is amazing how down to earth He is as a Father.

Continuing the discussion about the man Job, we saw that Job was given so much by God and that as a result, he had a touch of pride. What Job was not aware of was that the devil had tried in the past to see how he can attack him but he discovered that God had built a hedge around Job. What this means is that God had prospered Job with material possessions and had blessed the works of his hands. It means also that God had so very well protected Job on every side that the devil could not get to him or touch him but because God saw pride in Job, He had to judge that pride. Again, it was actually God who alerted the devil or brought Job back to the devil's attention!

In other words, as a result of the pride that God saw in Job, He personally delivered Job to the devil for a season so that the devil will bring him to nothing and then God can rebuild him in the way that He wants him — one with a humble heart. As a result, what Job's story teaches us is to watch out for those who might be seemingly well setup and prospering but have enthroned themselves in their own eyes. As you know, God does not tolerate rivalry; He is jealous. He says, "I am a jealous God, I will not share my glory with any other or with graven images." Therefore, you cannot touch His glory.

When you approach God with your own self-righteousness and God wants to deal with it, God has to bring some form of correction to you because one of His duties is to abase pride. The problem was not that Job was not righteous because he was righteous according to God's standard of righteousness in his days but what we have to remember is that pride always goes before a fall according to **Proverbs 16:18**:

> **"Pride goeth before destruction,** and **an haughty spirit before a fall"**

In **Job 9:32-35** we again see Job complaining about God and saying that he and God needed to come together in judgment and that **they needed to have someone lay hands on both of their shoulders to settle their matter. He treated God as his equal**:

> "For he is not a man, as I am, that I should answer him, and we should come together in judgment. 33 **Neither is there any <u>daysman</u>** (mediator) **betwixt us, <u>that might lay his hand upon us both</u>.** 34 Let him take his rod away from me, and let not his fear terrify me: 35 Then would I speak, and not fear him; but it is not so with me."

A lot of us are not different from Job whenever the rubber meets the road in our lives. Many people judge God as being unfair while leaning on their own self-righteousness. Just like Job, these types of people charge God foolishly as well. As I said before, they blame Him because He did not do what they wanted Him to do when they wanted Him to do it. Therefore to them, God has been unfair. In **Job 38:2-18** we see what God had to say to Job and all the likes of Job who claim to "know-it-all":

> **"Who is this that darkeneth counsel by words without knowledge?** *3* **Gird up now thy loins like a man; for I will demand of thee, and answer thou me.** *4* Where wast thou when I laid the foundations of the earth? declare, if thou hast understanding... *17* **Have the gates of death been opened unto thee? or hast thou seen the doors of the shadow of death?** *18* **Hast thou perceived the breadth of the earth?** declare if thou knowest it all."

This is God talking not just to Job but to all the "know-it-alls" in the world that are just like Job. What He wants to know is, "Do you have an answer to all these questions in the scriptures above as well as the questions in the scriptures immediately below before you all started shooting off your mouths?" God will go after those shooting their mouths off at Him because He hates pride. God is displeased with those who ignorantly charge Him foolishly instead of seeking Him for answers and this is evident in the way He continues His questioning of the "know-it-alls" in **Job 38:19-41**:

> **"Where is the way where light dwelleth? and as for darkness, where is the place thereof,** *20* That thou shouldest take it to the bound thereof, and that thou shouldest know the paths to the house thereof? *21* **Knowest thou**

**it, because thou wast then born? or because the number of thy days is great?** *(God has always been from eternity)* **22 Hast thou entered into the treasures of the snow? or hast thou seen the treasures of the hail,**

**23 Which I have reserved against the time of trouble, against the day of battle and war? 24 By what way is the light parted, which scattereth the east wind upon the earth? 25 Who hath divided a watercourse for the overflowing of waters, or a way for the lightning of thunder;** 26 To cause it to rain on the earth, where no man is; on the wilderness, wherein there is no man; 27 To satisfy the desolate and waste ground; and to cause the bud of the tender herb to spring forth?

*28* **Hath the rain a father? or who hath begotten the drops of dew?** *29* **Out of whose womb came the ice? and the hoary frost of heaven, who hath gendered it?** *30* The waters are hid as with a stone, and the face of the deep is frozen. *31* Canst thou bind the sweet influences of Pleiades, or loose the bands of Orion? *32* Canst thou bring forth Mazzaroth in his season? or canst thou guide Arcturus with his sons?

*33* **Knowest thou the ordinances of heaven? canst thou set the dominion thereof in the earth?** *34* **Canst thou lift up thy voice to the clouds, that abundance of waters may cover thee?** *35* **Canst thou send lightnings, that they may go, and say unto thee, Here we are?** *36* **Who hath put wisdom in the inward parts? or who hath given understanding to the heart?** *37* Who can number the clouds in wisdom? or who can stay the bottles of heaven,

*38* When the dust groweth into hardness, and the clods cleave fast together? *39* **Wilt thou hunt the prey for the lion? or fill the appetite of the young lions, *40* When they couch in their dens, and abide in the covert to lie in wait? *41* Who provideth for the raven his food? when his young ones cry unto God, they wander for lack of meat."**

We can now see Job's humility in the scripture below as he calls himself **vile.** This is a long way for one who had regarded himself so highly in the following words, "I chose out their way, and sat chief, and dwelt as a king in the army, as one that comforteth the mourners." We see Job's new found humility in his reply to God in **Job 40:4-5:**

"**Behold, I am vile; what shall I answer thee? I will lay mine hand upon my mouth.** *5* Once have I spoken; but I will not answer: yea, twice; but I will proceed no further."

And also in **Job 42:3-6** as he again declared:

"Who is he that hideth counsel without knowledge? **therefore have I uttered that I understood not; things too wonderful for me, which I knew not**... *5* I have heard of thee by the hearing of the ear: but now mine eye seeth thee. *6* **Wherefore I abhor myself, and repent in dust and ashes.** "

As you can see, Job is now willing to acknowledge his ignorance and the fact that he has been speaking from a very lofty point of view and he repented. We should all be like Job and humble ourselves before God lest He comes to abase the pride that He sees in us. From this encounter with Job, we see an aspect of God's supremacy on earth so that before anyone of us chooses to shoot off his or her mouth to charge Him foolishly, we can be fully aware of whom we are dealing with.

Again, Job thought that he was so righteous and that God had unjustly treated him wrong. He had also said, "If I am tried, I am going to come forth as gold." **It is true that Job was righteous but God was not dealing with his righteousness but with his lofty ideas about himself and He wanted to humble him.** The bottom line is that God came to bring to abasement the pride that He saw in Job so that He can bless Job with more.

The problem that God had with Job was that before He could give Job more, He first needed to remove pride from Job's life. God was determined to remove the things that made Job to feel high and lofty and God used the devil to accomplish the task. This is why He was not pleased with Job's friends in **Job 42:7-8** because they questioned Job's righteousness and misrepresented God before Job:

> **"And it was so, that after the LORD had spoken these words unto Job, the LORD said to Eliphaz the Temanite, My wrath is kindled against thee, and against thy two friends: <u>for ye have not spoken of me the thing that is right, as my servant Job hath.</u>**
>
> *8* **Therefore take unto you now seven bullocks and seven rams, <u>and go to my servant Job, and offer up for yourselves a burnt offering; and my servant Job shall pray for you: for him will I accept</u>: lest I deal with you after your folly, in that ye have not spoken of me the thing which is right, like my servant Job."**

Although Job was blaming God for his trials, still when he was squeezed with all the evil unleashed against him by the devil, he did not lose sight of the need to hold on to his righteousness. God called him His servant twice in the above scripture. What this tells us is that God came to make Job a better man and not to destroy him.

Again, to God, Job had a little touch of pride just like Joseph the son of Jacob had with his preppy multi-color coat and God was determined to process them both so that they could be of use to Him. In the case of Joseph, He saw Joseph walking about in his prideful state and God needed all of it to be dusted off of Joseph so He allowed his brothers to take him on a painful wicked journey into Egypt.

## Knowing God as the Righteous Judge

Judgment is always God's last resort when a person has become totally rebellious against Him. As I stated in the previous chapter, when a person consistently tells Him that he or she is not willing to change and God watches as the person's "cup of iniquity" fills up, then God will bring His judgment on that person when their cup is full. God wants us all to constantly empty our "cups of iniquity" by repenting of our sins but if we allow them to fill up without repentance, then we leave Him no choice but to bring His judgment on the scene because **He is a Righteous Judge**. He has to move in judgment because He is a judge. He is a Holy God and He metes out righteous judgments!

Look at what He said to David in **2 Samuel 7:12-14** right after He promised to bless David's son Solomon and to prosper Solomon as the next king after his father King David:

> "And when thy days be fulfilled, and thou shalt sleep with thy fathers, I will set up thy seed after thee *(Solomon)*, which shall proceed out of thy bowels, and I will establish his kingdom. *13* He shall build an house for my name, and I will stablish the throne of his kingdom forever. *14* I will be his father, and he shall be my son. **If he**

**commit iniquity, I will chasten him with the <u>rod of men</u>, and with <u>the stripes of the children of men</u>."**

As I stated before, just because a person is blessed by God or has been prospered by God does not mean that He will overlook the person's iniquities or sins. True to His Word about His punishment if Solomon commits iniquity, when Solomon sinned against Him by building alters of idolatry for his foreign wives and also by allowing them to sway him away from the Only Living and One True God, He stirred up the son of the King of Edom, **Hadad** to go after Solomon.

He also stirred up **Rezon** who reigned over Damascus and Syria as well as **Jeroboam** in Israel. **Hadad** and **Rezon** went to war against the house of Solomon and God gave **Jeroboam** 10 of the 12 tribes of Israel and He only left one tribe (Benjamin) for the house of Solomon in addition to the tribe of Judah. The only reason He left the one tribe was because He wanted to honor David's faithfulness and keep His promise to David — **1 Kings 11:14-33.** Yes, when needed, God will use the **"rod of men"** and the **"stripes of the children of men"** to chasten those who commit sins and iniquities as demonstrated in the case of King Solomon:

> **"And the LORD stirred up an adversary unto Solomon, Hadad the Edomite:** he was of the king's seed in Edom... 23 **And God <u>stirred him up</u> <u>another adversary</u>, Rezon the son of Eliadah**... 24 And he gathered men unto him, and became captain over a band, when David slew them of Zobah: and they went to Damascus, and dwelt therein, and reigned in Damascus. 25 **And he was an adversary to Israel all the days of Solomon, beside the mischief that Hadad did:** and he abhorred Israel, and reigned over Syria.

26 And **Jeroboam** the son of Nebat, an Ephrathite of Zereda, Solomon's servant, whose mother's name was Zeruah, a widow woman, **even he lifted up his hand against the king.** 27 **And this was the cause that he lifted up his hand against the king:** Solomon built Millo, and repaired the breaches of the city of David his father... 29 And it came to pass at that time when **Jeroboam** went out of Jerusalem, that **the prophet Ahijah** the Shilonite found him in the way; and he had clad himself with a new garment; and they two were alone in the field:

30 **And Ahijah caught the new garment that was on him, and rent it in twelve pieces:** 31 **And he said to Jeroboam, Take thee ten pieces: for thus saith the LORD, the God of Israel, Behold, I will rend the kingdom out of the hand of Solomon, and will give ten tribes to thee:** 32 (But he shall have one tribe for my servant David's sake, and for Jerusalem's sake, the city which I have chosen out of all the tribes of Israel:)

33 **Because that they have forsaken me, and have worshipped Ashtoreth the goddess of the Zidonians, Chemosh the god of the Moabites, and Milcom the god of the children of Ammon, and have not walked in my ways, to do that which is right in mine eyes, and to keep my statutes and my judgments, as did David his father."**

The house of David was already ruling over the tribe of Judah hence you saw the LORD God only counting 11 tribes when he gave 10 tribes to Jeroboam and one tribe (Benjamin) to the house of David in addition to the tribe of Judah that it already had.

As the **Righteous Judge**, we must know that God is the **last Court of Appeal** for mankind. Human beings might pervert or engage in a miscarriage of justice but God is always righteous in all His judgments. He will not pervert or engage in a miscarriage of justice neither will He prefer one person to another. He is **God-Almighty** and **He is love** but when you come to that place that He needs to judge you, He will pour out His righteous judgment on you no matter who you are and no matter how long you have been walking with Him.

The bottom line is that He hates sin and He will judge sin when He needs to. Therefore, we have to have a balanced understanding of the God that we are dealing with because there is a severe side to Him when it comes to His righteous judgments. When you look at His first act of judgment in the Garden of Eden, you will see that He does not condone sin nor accept excuses for someone's unwillingness or failure to repent because He always gives us the opportunity to repent.

For example, He already knew that Adam and Eve had sinned against Him but when He came on the scene, He simply asked Adam if he had disobeyed His commandment not to eat the fruit of the "Tree of the Knowledge of Good and Evil," but Adam blamed Eve rather repent as we can see in **Genesis 3:9-13. God gave both Adam and Eve the opportunity to repent by the way that He phrased His question to them:**

> "And the LORD God called unto Adam, and said unto him, **Where art thou?** *10* And he said, I heard thy voice in the garden, and I was afraid, because I was naked; and I hid myself. *11* And he said, <u>Who told thee that thou wast naked</u>? **Hast thou eaten of the tree, whereof I commanded thee that thou shouldest not eat**? *12* And the <u>man said</u>, **The woman whom thou gavest to be with me, she gave me of the tree,**

**and I did eat.** *13* And the LORD <u>God said unto the woman,</u> **What is this that thou hast done?** And the <u>woman said,</u> **The serpent beguiled me, and I did eat.**"

As you can clearly see, both Adam and Eve failed to take responsibilities for their actions and to acknowledge the fact that they had sinned against God. Instead, Adam blamed Eve and Eve blamed the serpent. Therefore, God had no choice as a righteous Judge but to bring forth His divine judgment against them as well as against the serpent in **Genesis 3:14-19:**

> *His Judgment on the Serpent*
> "And the <u>LORD God said unto the serpent,</u> **Because thou hast done this, thou art cursed above all cattle, and above every beast of the field; upon thy belly shalt thou go, and dust shalt thou eat all the days of thy life**: *15* <u>And I will put enmity between thee and the woman, and between thy seed and her seed; it shall bruise thy head, and thou shalt bruise his heel</u>."

The serpent and the woman had formed an ungodly alliance and the serpent used the woman to cause Adam to fall. In other words, as soon as Eve fell, the serpent immediately turned her into his vessel of devious dealings and Eve in compliance used the manipulative and seductive tactics that the devil taught her in order to make Adam agree to eat the fruit. God did not want their ungodly alliance to prosper so He put "enmity" between them and between their future generations. Therefore, the children of the devil will always war against the seed of the woman which is Christ:

> *His Judgment on Eve*
> "<u>Unto the woman he said,</u> **I will greatly multiply thy sorrow and thy conception; in sorrow thou shalt bring forth children; and thy desire shall**

**be to thy husband, and <u>he shall rule over thee</u>** *(she had usurped Adam's authority by persuading him to yield to her [become submissive to her] in eating the fruit she offered him; the fruit she knew very well that God told him not to eat)."*

Again, as you saw, the devil had immediately recruited Eve to help him destroy the man as soon as she fell and Eve complied. Together, they brought about Adam's fall. Only God knows the particular tactics that Eve used on Adam. Knowing how the devil operates and the way that he uses women, we can guess that manipulation and seduction was involved. This is why her judgment was tied to the pain of childbirth because she got Adam to yield through her seduction and sexual tactics. Her judgment reveals her sin:

### His Judgment on Adam

**"<u>And unto Adam he said,</u> Because thou hast hearkened unto <u>the voice of thy wife,</u> and hast eaten of the tree, of which <u>I commanded thee, saying, Thou shalt not eat of it:</u> <u>cursed is the ground for thy sake;</u> in sorrow shalt thou eat of it all the days of thy life;**

**18 Thorns also and thistles shall it bring forth to thee; and thou shalt eat the herb of the field; 19 In the sweat of thy face shalt thou eat bread, till thou return unto the ground; for out of it wast thou taken: for dust thou art, and unto dust shalt thou return."**

### An Analysis of the Judgments

God in His righteous judgment abased the serpent, re-subjected Eve back under Adam's authority and then judged the ground for Adam's sake. **This is one of the finest judgments displayed by God in scriptures. Adam had allowed his wife to usurp his authority and had become subjected both to**

Eve and the devil by his single act of yielding to obey his wife Eve rather correct or rebuke her. **God had to correct the new "ungodly authority structure" between Adam and Eve by placing Eve right back under Adam's authority;** hence He said to Eve, **"and he shall <u>rule</u> over thee."**

**This "ungodly authority structure" is still a problem for the man today when God's Word is not adhered to in the home because the woman without guidance by the Word of God, can still easily take authority away from the man who himself is not subject to the Word of God.** It is one of the reasons for broken marriages today because the men feel that their wives do not allow them to be "the man" or "the head of the household." **The devil used Eve to carry out a coup d'état against all men (represented by Adam) way back in the garden so you can see why God had to bring Eve back under Adam's authority.**

<u>As for Adam, God could not bring a curse or a judgment directly upon Adam because Adam was partly from Him and partly from the earth</u>. Remember that He made Adam from a lump of clay and He breathed His own breath into the clay? Well, His breath (Spirit) is the very life in Adam. **Therefore, to avoid placing a curse on Himself, He placed the curse on the earth so that the part of Adam that was from the earth will then receive the curse.** How great is God's wisdom and judgment!

We must never forget or lose sight of the fact that God is a Righteous Judge. Just because He comes to our aid and shows us mercy when we are in trouble or in pain is no reason to neglect this aspect of who He is. He knows that we are helpless without Him but helping us does not prevent Him from doing the necessary work in us to keep us on the right path or to make us spiritually strong.

There are times that I have cried out to Him about a situation and He would come on the scene and actually cry with me just to let me know that He cares about what happens to me and about how I feel. But, because He is determined that I go through the process so that His desired work will be accomplished in me, He does not just make the situation go away. Instead, He gives me the grace and the wisdom to cope and overcome the situation.

A lot of times, what is needed is instruction about what to do. This aspect of Him used to baffle me because He would be right there with me talking to me and I know that He can make the situation go away just at the snap of His finger but instead, He tells me what to do. He knew that I was not pleased with this approach so one day He said to me, **"Warriors are made on the battlefield you know."** He continued by saying that **"No one sits in their living room and gets a phone call that he has been made a GENERAL without actually going to war!"** God will have His way in our lives when we cry out to Him for righteousness.

It might not be pleasant while we are going through His processing but at the end, we do come forth as gold. He loves us, He strengthens us and He also will judge us if we do not repent of our sins.

## *Chapter 6*
# Understanding the Wrath and the Fierce Side of God

### God Has a Hot Wrath

We will do well to know that there is a side of God that can wax hot in wrath according to His own Words in **Exodus 32:10.** He visits His wrath on those who rebel against Him and His Word. For instance, when the children of Israel consistently murmured and rebelled against Him and His authority structure in Moses, He wanted to consume them with His hot wrath:

> "**Now therefore let me alone** *(in other words, do not intercede for them)*, **that <u>my wrath may wax hot</u> against them, <u>and that I may consume them</u>**: and I will make of thee a great nation" (Exodus 32:10).

According to **1 Thessalonians 5:9**, no Christian is appointed to God's wrath because <u>God in Christ Jesus has delivered us from His wrath</u>. We can only walk in this promise if we are living by the Word of God:

> "**For God hath not appointed us to wrath, but to obtain salvation by our Lord Jesus Christ.**"

Again, no Christian will experience the wrath of God unless they willfully forsake God's Word and choose to live a life of sin. Those who serve Him with lip service will experience His wrath in abundance. **The Lord Jesus is the Ark of Safety from God's wrath** because when we come to God in Christ, He wipes away all our sins. Also, when we sin and genuinely repent of our sins, God forgives us rather than stir up His wrath against us as recorded in **Psalms 78:38**:

"But he, being full of compassion, forgave their iniquity, and destroyed them not: **yea, many a time turned he his anger away, and did not stir up all his wrath.**"

After a prolonged patience, God will pour out His wrath against those who rejected or transgressed His Word according to **Romans 1:18**:

"**For the wrath of God is revealed from heaven against all ungodliness and unrighteousness of men, who hold the truth** (*the Word of God*) **in unrighteousness.**"

When you anger God for a long period of time, He is capable of letting you experience His hot wrath as a form of His judgment against you. For instance, He judges those who choose to walk in cruelty towards others instead of walking in love. He will avenge those who are afflicted as stated in **Exodus 22:21-24**:

"<u>Thou shalt neither vex a stranger, nor oppress him: for ye were strangers in the land of Egypt.</u> 22 <u>Ye shall not afflict any widow, or fatherless child.</u> 23 <u>If thou afflict them in any wise, and they cry at all unto me,</u> **I will surely hear their cry;** 24 **And my wrath shall wax hot, and I will kill you with the sword; and your wives shall be widows, and your children fatherless.**"

### *An Account of God's Wrath on the Wicked*

*I once saw how God allowed someone to experience His wrath in a very dramatic way. During one of my visits to Nigeria, I had to take a bus home from somewhere and everyone paid a set fee before entering the bus. The bus was not quite full so the driver made three stops and picked up three male passengers and he charged them about half the normal fare. No one said anything to him because we were more than half way into the journey. On his fourth stop, a lady got into the bus and the driver charged her the full fare which was ₦5 (Naira) more than what he charged each of the last three male passengers.*

*There was an immediate out-cry from all the female passengers along with some of the male passengers. The driver refused to charge the woman what he had charged the last men claiming that it was his last trip for the day. To everyone's amazement, the lady said to him, "I am a child of God and I know that He will fight for me" and she told everyone to leave him alone and let God handle it. In response, the driver made a very rude comment to her. Unfortunately for this driver, God decided to avenge this lady instantly. In Nigeria at the time of this visit, there were a lot of police check-points on just about every main road in Lagos (the former capital of Nigeria). To me, these check-points were nothing but a way for the police officers to collect bribes from drivers; especially the commercial drivers.*

*Through the journey, I watched as the driver would reach into his pocket and place money in the hand of the police officer at each of these check-points. At the next check-point after he picked up this lady, the police officer on duty refused whatever amount he had slipped into his hands. He demanded more and I saw as he added a ₦5 to the amount. I said to myself, that was the ₦5 that he unfairly took from the lady and even the lady said to him, "Didn't I tell you that my God was going to fight for me?"*

*Apparently God was not done with the driver yet because when we got to the next check-point, he again offered some amount to the police officer on duty and the police officer said something to him and he made a rude remark to the officer. At this, the officer demanded that he park the bus on the side of the road and he then dragged him out of the bus. As this was going on, a van carrying some soldiers appeared from nowhere and they wanted to know what was going on and the police officer said something to them. They went over to the driver and I guess they did not like the way he talked to them when they tried to interrogate him.*

*All of a sudden they began to lash him with their cowhide whip called "koboko." Even after beating him, the soldiers were still not satisfied that they had disciplined him well enough so a couple of them got into the bus and told him to proceed to drop off the passengers at the next stop which was the last bus-stop and they were going to take him to jail for the night!*

*I was amazed at how God fought for this lady by sending more wicked people to deal with the wicked driver. It made me to remember what God said to David in 2 Samuel 7:14:*

> *"I will be his father, and he shall be my son. If he commit iniquity, I will chasten him with the rod of men, and with the stripes of the children of men."*

According to **Revelation 16:1**, God's end time wrath is reserved for all those that will not turn away from their wicked ways and live by God's Word. It states that, right after the time of the tribulation, God's end time wrath shall be poured out against all those who are ungodly:

> "And I heard a great voice out of the temple saying to the seven angels, Go your ways, **and pour out the vials of the wrath of God upon the earth**."

And also in **Ezekiel 38:19**:

> **"For in my jealousy and in the fire of my wrath have I spoken,** Surely in that day there shall be a great shaking in the land of Israel."

Knowing this aspect of God will help us to reverence Him as we ought. We want to know God's mercy and grace on a daily basis and we want to stay delivered in Christ Jesus from His wrath because He has not appointed us to His wrath. His wrath is for the wicked.

## God is a Refining Fire

We must know that although God is love, but at the same time this loving God is also a refining fire. **Also, we must be aware that God is a consuming fire to the wicked but His fire refines the righteous.** In other words, God is a consuming fire against the wicked and a refining fire to His children. Therefore, when we come to Him, He begins a process of burning sin out of our lives and He also begins to shake away anything that is not of Him in our lives. That is why when He comes into our lives, He sets fire to everything in our lives that is not like Him or that rivals Him in our lives. He begins to incinerate them and one by one we see our friends go and those around us begin to speak unkind things about us and we wonder what will be left after He is done with us. We learn about this refining fire side of God's nature in **Malachi 3:1-3**:

> "Behold, I will send my messenger, and he shall prepare the way before me: and the Lord, whom ye seek, shall suddenly come to his temple, even the messenger of the covenant, whom ye delight in: behold, he shall come, saith the LORD of hosts. 2 But who may abide the day of his coming? and who shall stand when he

appeareth? **for he is like a refiner's fire, and like fullers' soap:** 3 And he shall sit as a refiner and purifier of silver: and he shall purify the sons of Levi, and purge them as gold and silver, that they may offer unto the LORD an offering in righteousness."

God will keep after you until you feel as if everyone has abandoned you and that it is just Jesus that is left in your life. At this point when you feel as though you are at your rock bottom, God says, **"Yes, I have you where I want you. If anything needs to be built now, I will build it through you and it will be long lasting; lest you be like Job and think that you are a self-made king among others."** Remember that this was what Job's testing was about; to humble him. When God was done with him, even his friends who in the past dared not speak to him negatively because of his wealth began to speak against him.

They had an ample opportunity to tell Job just what they really thought of him as they reminded him of all the things that they had watched him do wrong. In summary, they told him that God brought all the evil against him because there was sin in his life. **It is the same way today, people will sing your praises when they think that you have something of value that they need but let any misfortune befall you and those same people that were crying, "Hosanna" for you will immediately begin to cry, "Crucify him"** just like the friends of Job.

This is part of man's fallen nature and it is why God does not want us to let any human being prop us up as a "demi-god." He wants to be the only one who builds us up and He wants us to have a solid foundation in Him. During your testing, you will be able to see as clearly as Job did that you are no chief or self-made king among your friends and that your prosperity and protection are from the Lord and not of your own making. I will talk more about how God works to cleanse us later in this chapter under the subtitle –**God is Our Purifier**.

## God is a Fierce Judge of Rebels and Instigators

God appointed the Levites as ministers before the congregation of the children of Israel because they were the sons and great grandsons of Levi. Although Aaron and his sons were also Levites, God separated them from the rest of the Levite ministers. He made Moses the deliverer, He made Aaron the High Priest and Aaron's sons Priests.

Due to man's fallen nature, greed and jealousy sometimes prevent people from appreciating what they have because they only focus on what they do not have that others have. Therefore, when you give them an inch, they want a mile as in the case of some Levites (Korah, Dathan and Abiram) who were Moses' main antagonists when Moses was leading the children of Israel through the wilderness.

As recorded in **Numbers 16:1-33**, Korah, Dathan and Abiram as the chief instigators in the camp recruited some of the other Levites to join them in their rebellion against Moses and against Aaron. It was not enough for Korah, Dathan and Abiram to be Levite ministers but they wanted to usurp Moses and Aaron's God-given positions of authority. This event is worth our attention because it shows us God's fierce anger and judgment.

**You must know this aspect of God because if you do not, you will think that just because you come into His throne room singing and praising Him that you can say and do things that disrespect His representatives or authority figures on earth. Korah, Dathan** and **Abiram** disrespected Moses and Aaron and God poured out His anger and judgment upon them in **Numbers 16:1-10:**

"Now **Korah,** the son of Izhar, the son of **Kohath,** the son of Levi, and **Dathan** and **Abiram,** the sons of Eliab, and On, the son of Peleth, sons of Reuben, took men: 2 **And they rose up before Moses, with certain of the children of Israel, two hundred and fifty princes of the assembly, famous in the congregation, men of renown:**

3 **And they gathered themselves together against Moses and against Aaron,** and said unto them, <u>Ye take too much upon you, seeing all the congregation are holy, every one of them, and the LORD is among them: wherefore then lift ye up yourselves above the congregation of the LORD?</u> 4 **And when Moses heard it, he fell upon his face:** 5 And he spake unto Korah and unto all his company, saying, <u>Even tomorrow the LORD will shew who are his, and who is holy;</u> and will cause him to come near unto him: even him whom he hath chosen will he cause to come near unto him...

8 And Moses said unto Korah *(the chief instigator),* Hear, I pray you, ye sons of Levi: 9 **Seemeth it but a small thing unto you, that the God of Israel hath separated you from the congregation of Israel, to bring you near to himself to do the service of the tabernacle of the LORD, and to stand before the congregation to minister unto them?** 10 <u>And he hath brought thee near to him, and all thy brethren the sons of Levi with thee:</u> **and seek ye the priesthood also?"**

It may seem to others that Moses and Aaron where exalting themselves above the congregation but it was God that placed them in their respective positions to lead the people and yes, to be heads of the congregation! I say again that it was God that made Moses the deliverer, Aaron the High Priest, Aaron's sons Priests and the other Levites Ministers. As the King over His creation, God sovereignly chose this authority structure over His kingdom and all were to obey it.

Because of their jealousy, Korah, Dathan and Abiram refused to accept this but began to create division in the camp by laying charges that Moses and Aaron were exalting themselves above the congregation. Moses then decided to resolve the problem that these instigators were creating in the camp by calling for a meeting with them in **Numbers 16:12-26** but they refused to come or to obey Moses:

> "And Moses sent to call **Dathan** and **Abiram**, the sons of Eliab: which said, **We will not come up**…
> *19* **And Korah gathered all the congregation against them unto the door of the tabernacle of the congregation**: and the glory of the LORD appeared unto all the congregation.
>
> *20* **And the LORD spake unto Moses and unto Aaron, saying,** *21* **Separate yourselves from among this congregation, that I may consume them in a moment…** 23 And the LORD spake unto Moses, saying, 24 Speak unto the congregation, saying, **Get you up from about the tabernacle of <u>Korah, Dathan, and Abiram</u>**.
>
> 25 And Moses rose up and went unto Dathan and Abiram; and the elders of Israel followed him. 26 **And he spake unto the congregation, saying, Depart, I pray you, from the tents of these wicked men, and touch nothing of theirs, lest ye be consumed in all their sins.**"

As you can see, God was willing to consume them in one moment as He told Moses, Aaron and the rest of the congregation to separate themselves from them so that He could consume them in a moment. Knowing that God was angry and about to judge the instigators, Moses said the following in **Numbers 16:28-33:**

> "And Moses said, Hereby ye shall know that the LORD hath sent me to do all these works; for I have not done them of mine own mind. *29* **If these men die the common death of all men, or if they be visited after the visitation of all men; then the LORD hath not sent me. *30* But if the LORD make a new thing, and the earth open her mouth, and swallow them up, with all that appertain unto them, and they go down quick into the pit; <u>then ye shall understand that these men have provoked the LORD</u>.**
>
> *31* <u>And it came to pass, as he had made an end of speaking all these words, that the ground clave asunder that was under them</u>: *32* **And the earth opened her mouth, and swallowed them up, and their houses, and all the men that appertained unto Korah, and all their goods. *33* They, and all that appertained to them, went down alive into the pit, and the earth closed upon them: and they perished from among the congregation."**

We do not hear sermons or teachings about this fierce side of God preached much these days because people are now being taught that they do not have to fear God because He is our father. They have reduced the teaching on the fear of God to only "the reverential fear of the Lord." Meaning that we are to now only **reverence** God but we are not to **fear** Him. To reverence someone means to have deep a respect or love for that person. Therefore, you can reverence a person without walking in fear of the person.

The fear of God on the other hand is to be aware of the fact that He alone can send you to hell forever if you live all your life in sin. **Fear denotes the presence of dread or apprehension** and God meant for it to help us depart from a life of sin. Thinking about the consequences of hell is really supposed to scare us straight because hell is real, just as heaven is real. God is going to send the sinners or the ungodly to hell and there will never be anyone that can get them out of there. The Bible calls it damnation.

What those who teach the doctrines of not having to fear God forget is that the only time that the Lord Jesus taught us to **fear** or **fear anyone** was when He told us to **fear God**. Before this time, the Lord always taught the disciples not to fear but when it comes to God in **Luke 12:4-5**, He told them who to fear. Yes, He told the disciples not to fear those that can only kill the body and after that cannot do anything more but that they must fear God because it is only God that can kill and destroy the human soul and body in hell forever:

> "And I say unto you my friends, Be not afraid of them that kill the body, and after that have no more that they can do. 5 **But I will forewarn you whom ye shall fear: Fear him, which after he hath killed hath power to cast into hell; yea, I say unto you, Fear him**."

It is a great thing to reverence God but beyond that, **we must always walk in the remembrance that He is the ultimate Judge and that when He rightly damns a soul to hell, there is no other Court of Appeal. It is the reason why we must fear Him beyond just reverencing Him.** We must fear Him enough to stay away from evil so that He does not judge and condemn us on Judgment Day. This is also why the Bible says in **Proverbs 8:13** that:

> "**The fear of the LORD is to hate evil: pride, and arrogancy, and the evil way,** and the froward mouth, do I hate."

Also take a look at the following scriptures and you will see what King Solomon said under the Anointing about the fear of the Lord in **Proverbs 14:27:**

> **"The fear of the LORD is a fountain of life, to depart from the snares of death."**

And David in **Psalms 111:10:**

> **"The fear of the LORD is the beginning of wisdom..."**

It is the knowledge of this fierce aspect of God's ability to utterly consume and destroy a person in hell that helps us not to sin against Him. We must also be careful to honor the legitimate authority and the hierarchy that He has setup on earth. Therefore, if God has not showed you something about His authority figure and has not given you instructions concerning them, do not take it upon yourself to rise up against them.

### God's Judgment of Aaron and Miriam's Insubordination

We will do well not to provoke God to anger by our words and our actions because His fierce anger can be visited on a person or on a people in so many different ways. Not many people take the time to study scriptures in order to understand the anger or the wrath of God. God can be tolerant and longsuffering but when He is provoked to anger, He can mete out fierce judgments.

Remember Miriam; Moses' older sister and how she was judged fiercely by God when she and Aaron spoke against Moses' authority and provoked God to anger? They had prejudice against the Ethiopian woman that Moses married. In other words, Moses married a black woman and they felt that because they were older than Moses and because God sometimes speaks to them also that they too can question Moses' authority. In doing so, they provoked God to anger and God's anger was unleashed by their words as recorded in **Numbers 12:1-11**:

> "**And Miriam and Aaron spake against Moses because of the Ethiopian woman whom he had married: for he had married an Ethiopian woman.** 2 And they said, **Hath the LORD indeed spoken <u>only by Moses</u>? hath he not spoken also by us? <u>And the LORD heard it.</u>** 3 (Now the man Moses was very meek, above all the men which were upon the face of the earth.)

> 4 **And the <u>LORD spake suddenly unto Moses,</u> and <u>unto Aaron</u>, and <u>unto Miriam</u>, Come out ye three unto the tabernacle of the congregation.** And they three came out. 5 And the LORD came down in the pillar of the cloud, and stood in the door of the tabernacle, **and called Aaron and Miriam: and they both came forth.**

> 6 <u>And he said, Hear now my words: If there be a prophet among you, I the LORD will make myself known unto him in a vision, and will speak unto him in a dream.</u> 7 **My servant Moses is not so, who is faithful in all mine house.** 8 **With him will I speak mouth to mouth, even apparently, and not in dark speeches; and the similitude of the LORD shall he behold: <u>wherefore then were ye not afraid to speak against my servant Moses?</u>** 9 **<u>And the anger of the LORD was kindled against them; and he departed.</u>**

> 10 **And the cloud departed from off the tabernacle; and, <u>behold, Miriam</u> became**

**leprous, white as snow**: and Aaron looked upon Miriam, and, behold, she was leprous. *11* **And Aaron said unto Moses, Alas, <u>my lord</u>, I beseech thee, lay not the sin upon us, wherein we have done foolishly, and wherein we have sinned**."

God's anger and judgment against Miriam made Aaron to remember that it was God that had set Moses up as the authority over him and you can see him now referring to Moses as **Lord** towards the end of the above scripture. We must be careful to honor He whom God has honored. This does not mean that we have to allow ourselves to be swindled, coerced, deceived, or manipulated by questionable "ministers" but to find out what God's Word says and to do it. Due to some of the questionable behaviors of some "ministers" today, we have to learn to take to the Lord in prayer what we see and what we hear about them so that He can tell us what to do and say.

In today's ministering environment, there are times that you may have to "overcome" the very "ministers" that were supposed to be God's overseers over you. Many "ministers" have tried to use their positions to stifle, control, manipulate or hinder those that are under them as they strive to build "their ministries." As a result, we have to be very discerning in order to identify God's true ministers and to discern the particular minister that God wants you to be under.

There are some things that can be obvious about a person's character because God has given us common sense and wisdom and we are to use them according to His Word to keep us from being deceived. Even the Lord Jesus forewarned us about the coming of some false prophets. We are to take heed that they do not deceive us by their sleek preaching and fund raising tactics that are ungodly. **My advice is to know the Word of God and use it to analyze**

**what you see and what you hear.** This way, you can keep from touching God's true prophets and from being deceived by the unscrupulous "ministers."

## God is Our Purifier

God uses our afflictions to refine and purify us and to make us know the difference between that which is holy and that which unholy. He declared to us in **Isaiah 48:10-11** that He actually chose the furnace of affliction as the place to purify and refine us:

> **"Behold, I have refined thee, but not with silver; <u>I have chosen thee in the furnace of affliction.</u>** *11* For mine own sake, even for mine own sake, will I do it: for how should my name be polluted? and I will not give my glory unto another."

God is willing to purify us with the fierce fire of afflictions if it is what it will take to make us shift from the place of rebellion or stubbornness. We see this in the case of the children of Israel who kept disobeying His Word about not worshipping idols and breaking His Sabbath. A time came that He delivered them up to their enemies for 70 years!:

> **"But after that our fathers had provoked the God of heaven unto wrath, he gave them into the hand of Nebuchadnezzar the king of Babylon, the Chaldean, who destroyed this house, and carried the people away into Babylon"** (Ezra 5:12).

To God, if it took 70 years of afflictions in Babylon for the children of Israel to learn to obey God's commandments in order for them stay away from idolatry and to become true worshippers of the One and Only Living God, He was willing to let them go through 70 years of afflictions and He did. As I stated before, He is the God that will take you to a land full of scorpions and serpents and He will let you know that He designed the route especially for you.

By this I mean that He will take you for example, to that office where nobody can stand you and He says to you, "I brought you here because I want you to love them; I chose you for this purpose and I want you to shine in this place because there is no light here. I want you to be the light." Meanwhile, you are praying for Him to please deliver you from the people because they cannot stand you and they speak against you constantly. You tell yourself that if not for these people, your life will be very good and in response, God says to you, "You do not understand; I brought you to this place; you are not here by accident."

I remember my experience in one of the places where I worked and how that my immediate manager was very driven and very hash towards me as well as towards others. Prior to my working in this company, I had witnessed the Lord defend and protect me against mean employers, managers and fellow employees when I cried out to Him in prayer. Therefore, when this lady became my manager, I knew to pray because I had watched the way she treated the people that were previously under her. By the fifth month of being under this woman, I begin to pray some 911 prayers to the Lord to remove her as my manger just as He had done in the past.

I mean, I previously saw God move my entire office unit out of Atlanta to another state just to get rid of those that troubled me! One of the mangers confessed that she knew that the dissolution of the particular branch of the company was as a result of my prayers to God about the office and about their actions. Therefore, because of God's move on my behalf in the past, I began to pray for God to also remove this new manager. I prayed about this particular manager for several months and nothing happened; to be point that I was troubled about the Lord's silence on the matter.

Then one day, the Lord sent me a prophetess that had the Word of the Lord for me and without my telling her about my work situation, she said to me, "The Lord said that He heard your prayers about removing your immediate manager but that **He will not remove her because He sent her as a 'chisel' to you and that He is using her to carve a beautiful sculpture!**" I was shocked to learn that this seemingly evil woman was one of God's carving instruments and boy, she was good at it.

Still, I was not pleased with the Word so I took it up with the Lord for confirmation and true to His Word; He told me point blank that as ungodly as the woman might be, she was not going anywhere. He showed me a vision of several infant carriers (baby Christians) lined up in an office in this particular company that this woman was an instrument to help God carve. Was she evil? Absolutely, but He chose her as a vessel that He used to teach me how to love — to love the unlovable. He told me to love her and to pray for her well being because love grows where there is none. It was not what I wanted to hear but He was right.

From that day, my attitude towards her changed as I began to see her as God's chisel; my specially sent chisel from the Lord. Also, according to the instruction from the Lord, I began to pray for her and not too long after that, God moved me to a better job with another company. God will always find a way to purify us even when it means using wicked people to set us straight. Remember that He used the devil to humble Job.

## God Declares the Ending from the Beginning
Below is what God Almighty said about Himself in **Isaiah 46:9-10** on this subject:

"<u>Remember the former things of old: for I am
God, and there is none else; I am God, and there
is none like me,</u> 10 **Declaring the end from the
beginning, and from ancient times the things
that are not yet done,** saying, My counsel shall
stand, and I will do all my pleasure."

Not only does God declare the ending of a matter from the
beginning, He also calls the "things that be not as though
they were." In other words, He is able to speak what He
desires into being even when they do not yet exist because
He is the creator of all substances. We see this alluded to in
**Romans 4:17:**

"...God, who quickeneth the dead, and
**calleth those things which be not as though
they were.**"

In Chapter 5 of this book, I wrote about how God told
Abraham that his descendants will be enslaved in a foreign
land for 400 years and that after that He will deliver them
and bring them back to the land of Canaan and He did. God
sees all things and He also sees what will happen in the
future. For instance, He already knows who will be saved
and who will be damned. He is able to do this because of
who He is but this knowledge does not prevent Him from
trying to save everyone by the preaching of the Gospel.
Below is my personal experience of how God declared the
ending from the beginning in my life:

### How God Declared Who I Was
*Before I finally got saved, I had become agnostic (not sure if
God exists or not) and I did not think that I had any time for
religion, church or Christians. Sunday was my day of rest
and I did not own a Bible but after my salvation experience,
I set out to correct my wrong beliefs and to learn about
God. I promptly went out and bought 12 Bibles in one day*

*but I did not read them much. For example, the layout of the Dake's Bible was confusing to me so, I immediately set it aside and never opened it again.*

*I had not learned the importance of the Word of God yet. Meanwhile, my sister saw that I was still holding on to my Roman Catholic traditions even after becoming born again. To correct this, she told me that the Roman Catholic Church's "Stations of the Cross" (the prayer stations during the month of lent) and the Rosary were not in the Bible and I did not believe her. She did not want to argue about it so we dropped the matter.*

*When I was by myself one day, the Holy Spirit said to me, "Don't you want to find out if your sister was right?" It was then that I remembered my sister's words about the Rosary and the "Stations of the Cross" so I set out to prove her wrong. I picked up a Bible, not to read the Gospel in order to understand the Lord's teachings but to look for where the "Stations of the Cross" and the Rosary were mentioned. As a result, I only scanned through Matthew Mark, Luke and John and I did not read much of the Old Testament or any of the Epistles so my understanding of the Word of the Lord was very limited.*

*This limited knowledge of the Word of the Lord proved not to be very good for me because about 7 months after becoming born again, I wound up in the psychiatric hospital in New York. I was having visions of the Lord Jesus, God the Father, the Holy Spirit, the devil, etc. The devil's harassments escalated to demonic attacks and as a result, I wound up in the psychiatric hospital. While in the psychiatric hospital, I was still seeing the Lord and <u>He would say to me</u>, **"You are the light of the world. A city that is set on a hill cannot be hid"** and to be honest with you, I had no idea what He was talking about. Even after I read the scripture where it was stated, I still could not*

155

*relate to it because sitting in the psychiatric hospital at the time, I did not feel like **"the light of the world"** neither did I feel like I was **"a city set on a hill."***

*I cried a lot and prayed all the time in my room within the four walls of that psychiatric ward and each time; His response to my cry was to repeat the same words, **"You are the light of the world. A city set on a hill cannot be hid."** I did not know what to make of His response to me and I would say to myself, what in the world is He talking about? I am sitting in a psychiatric ward locked up and the devil is telling me that He is going to make sure that they lock me up forever and throw away the key and the Lord is talking about the light of the world and a city that is set on a hill. To me, the words did not match my situation at the time because what I wanted was deliverance from the psychiatric ward and the hospital.*

I again looked up the scripture in **Matthew 5:14-16** that He spoke to me and because I lacked the understanding of it, His response to my cry still did not seem appropriate to me. You can read it for yourself below:

*"**Ye are the light of the world. A city that is set on an hill cannot be hid.** 15 Neither do men light a candle, and put it under a bushel, but on a candlestick; and it giveth light unto all that are in the house. 16 **Let your light so shine before men, that they may see your good works, and glorify your Father which is in heaven."***

At first, I did not even know that this scripture was in the Bible before He quoted it. **At the time, did I feel like a city sitting on a hill in the inside of a psychiatric ward? Did I feel like a light in any place? No, but He said that I was and He knew what He was talking about.** He can declare the ending from the beginning. It took me almost two years to catch on to what He told me then. When I finally caught on to what He meant, it still felt far-fetched. I knew that I had to make a serious effort to understand Him, and I had to understand His Word so that I can have a better idea of His ways and what He expects from me.

From His perspective, He saw my future and as a result was determined to rid me of all my agnostic beliefs and thinking that had allowed the devil and his evil spirits to manifest themselves to me in order to afflict me. According to Him, He allowed the drastic measure of demonic afflictions and the time in the psychiatric hospital to cure me of my agnosticism. I am now fully persuaded that He exists and I know that the devil and his evil spirits also exist but it took God allowing the devil to have a "go at me" to shock me into reality. I know first-hand that God is a master strategist so He knows where to take each one of us in order for Him to accomplish His desires concerning us.

Today, books that He has given me to write and sermons that He has given me to preach along with His spiritual insights and wisdom that He manifests through me by His Spirit really help to light up the dark places in many people's lives. He declared the ending from the beginning in my life and I can see His light shinning brighter through me every day. The very end is not yet.

## *Chapter 7*
# Understanding the Meaning of the Word GOD

According to the Lord, many of us do not really understand what it means when we say the word **GOD**. We do not know the true meaning of the word. **He told me that only Job knew the true definition of the word GOD in his days.** If you were told to sit and to write the meaning of the word **GOD** today, what would you write? What do you understand the word **GOD** to mean? Because we cannot accurately define the meaning of **GOD**, the devil spends a great deal of his time challenging the meaning of it in our lives using adverse situations or circumstances. When you can define accurately what it means for God to be GOD, you will gain a wider perspective about His ways, His sovereignty, and His kingdom rules and you can put the devil beneath your feet where he belongs.

## Knowing the Sovereignty of God

Many people reject Him, curse Him and make rude remarks about Him because of something that happened in their lives for which they blame Him. As you begin to learn the true definition of God, you will discover that He can be anything that is good that you want Him to be in your life. We have already established that He is everywhere and He sees all things and knows all things. **You must also know that He has no faults, He cannot be blamed, He cannot fail, He does not change, and that He can make a sovereign decision about anything or anyone at any time on planet earth.**

As I said before, there is a drastic side of God that most people never think about or become aware of and as a result, they "miss-define" who God really is. You must know that for your own good, He can come into your life and take away anything and everything that you have set up as an idol in your life. He is the God that owns everything and does not tolerate idols; He can take your children or that thing that you have set up as your little Isaac. Yes, He can take it away. You can cry twenty years and it will not make a difference.

It is not because He does not care about you but it is because He cares for you too much to let idolatry destroy you and it does not matter the nature of the idol. He removes all idols especially when we cry out to Him to purify and sanctify us. Remember what He said and did to the Prophet Ezekiel in **Ezekiel 24:15-18**? In essence this is what He told Ezekiel, "Your wife has become too precious in your sight and she has become an idol in your life. Therefore, I am going to take her away with a stroke of my hand and you are not to cry about it."

> "Also the word of the LORD came unto me, saying, *16* **Son of man, behold, I take away from thee** <u>the desire of thine eyes with a stroke:</u> **yet neither shalt thou mourn nor weep, neither shall thy tears run down.** *17* <u>Forbear to cry, make no mourning for the dead, bind the tire of thine head upon thee, and put on thy shoes upon thy feet, and cover not thy lips, and eat not the bread of men.</u> *18* **So I spake unto the people in the morning: and at even my wife died; and I did in the morning as I was commanded"** (Ezekiel 24:15-18).

Can you imagine that in your life? God coming one day and making a vital decision as in the case of Ezekiel and you have to keep serving and praising Him because He is God? I will tell you that this is one of the ways that the Prophet Ezekiel acquired the true definition of what it means for God to be God in his life. It was how Job also leaned the true definition of God. Knowing that He owns everything and that all souls are His and a result, He can make a sovereign decision concerning any soul at any time without prior permission from anyone — He is God!:

**"Behold, all souls are mine; as the soul of the father, so also the soul of the son is mine: <u>the soul that sinneth, it shall die</u>"** (Ezekiel 18:4).

Also, when God killed Aaron's children in **Leviticus 10:1-7,** He told Aaron not to mourn because of the Anointing that was upon his life:

> **"And Nadab and Abihu, the sons of Aaron, took either of them his censer, and put fire therein, and put incense thereon, and offered strange fire before the LORD, which he commanded them not. 2 And there went out fire from the LORD, and devoured them, and they died before the LORD.** 3 Then Moses said unto Aaron, <u>This is it that the LORD spake, saying, I will be sanctified in them that come nigh me, and before all the people I will be glorified.</u> **And Aaron held his peace...**
>
> 6 And Moses said unto Aaron, and unto Eleazar and unto Ithamar, his sons, **Uncover not your heads, neither rend your clothes; lest ye die, and lest wrath come upon all the people: but let your brethren, the whole house of Israel, bewail the burning which the LORD hath kindled. 7 And ye shall not go out from the door of the tabernacle of the congregation, lest ye die: <u>for the anointing oil of the LORD is upon you</u>.** <u>And they did according to the word of Moses."</u>

**Many people do not know God as the sovereign ruler who makes the final decision concerning us and concerning everything on earth. Therefore, when our desires or our plans clash with His, we react towards Him negatively.** We must know that as God, He does not need anyone's approval or permission when He makes a sovereign decision but what we need to know is that even His seemingly drastic, and painful decisions are for our own good.

He loves us and He will do whatever is needed (all His works are in righteousness) so that we can succeed in His plans for us. He does not intend evil towards us but good. He declared this in **Jeremiah 29:11**:

> "For I know the thoughts that I think toward you, saith the LORD, **thoughts of <u>peace</u>, and <u>not of evil</u>, to give you <u>an expected end</u>**."

Actually, we are the ones who set up things that we think are good for us and He comes in to remove them because He sees the destructive end of those things. Therefore, it is in our best interest to always remind ourselves that everything under the whole of heaven is His. Your son is His, your daughter is His, your mother is His, and everything that you think you have labored for and stored in the bank or other secret places are all His and He can make a sovereign decision about them at any time.

Therefore, you have to acquaint yourself with the sovereignty of God. **He can sovereignly take you on a journey that He designed for you and He can sovereignly remove from you all those things that were "gods" in your life before you accepted Him into your life and He will bring you to the place where you understand that you are to hang onto every word that He says to you.** He must make you to understand that your life is not about your bank account, your children, your reputation, etc., but about Him.

The Lord Jesus demonstrated to us that God is the Sovereign owner of all things when He sent His disciples to go get Him an ass and a colt in **Matthew 21:1-7**. He told them that **if any man should ask why they are taking it, they**

**should just tell the person that the Lord has need of it.** You and I know that if it was another person who sent people to go and to take someone else's colt or ass, the person would have been arrested for stealing. This clearly shows the power of the Lord's Words because once they said that the Lord has need of the ass and the colt, no one bothered them:

> "And when they drew nigh unto Jerusalem, and were come to Bethphage, unto the mount of Olives, then sent Jesus two disciples, 2 Saying unto them, **Go into the village over against you, and straightway ye shall find an ass tied, and a colt with her: loose them, and bring them unto me. 3 And if any man say ought unto you, ye shall say, The Lord hath need of them; and straightway he will send them.**
>
> 4 All this was done, that it might be fulfilled which was spoken by the prophet, saying, 5 Tell ye the daughter of Sion, Behold, thy King cometh unto thee, meek, and sitting upon an ass, and a colt the foal of an ass. 6 **And the disciples went, and did as Jesus commanded them, 7 And brought the ass, and the colt, and put on them their clothes, and they set him thereon.**"

As you can see, He has the final Word concerning even our material possessions.


## We Came in with Nothing and We Leave with Nothing

Once He told me not to place too much emphasis on material things because they all belong to Him. According to Him, we all met all the material things here on earth and whenever we leave, we must leave them all behind whether we like it or not. In other words, we met them here and we must leave them here when we exit the earth.

We cannot take anything with us out of this world. He told me that if I do not believe Him that **I should take a look at a child that has just been born and a person that has just died and is about to be buried. According to Him, the one thing that they have in common is NOTHING; they have nothing. One brought in nothing and the other is going out with nothing no matter how rich he was in his lifetime.** Therefore, I am to always remember that everything on earth belongs to Him and not to waste my life in trying to own them because He has set it up so that no one brings anything into the world and no one takes anything out of here.

**This is the whole purpose of why He allows us to be tested so that we can see things from His perspective and it is very painful because we are very dependent beings. We depend on people, on money, on our jobs, on our reputation, etc.** Therefore, a person can get a job and after some years of getting paid on a regular basis, it becomes the person's source and security; then God tells the person to give it up. Yes, if the person is spirit filled and hungers for more of God, He can sometimes demand the things you hold most dear like your job, your money, your time, your friends, your reputation, etc. Yes, God comes on the scene and tells you what you must give up.

All of a sudden, your knees begin to buckle as you remind God about your wife or your husband, your children, your mortgage, your other family responsibilities and so forth. You will start having the following types of conversation with Him about your spouse saying, *"Let me tell You about my wife or my husband. He or she will not understand when I say that You told me to do this. He or she likes the bank account and having money to pay the bills on time and You are telling me to leave this job?"* In response, He says again to you, "Leave it and follow me."

These types of experiences make you begin to have an appreciation for people like Abraham. For instance, Abraham did not know the land of Canaan; he had no idea where Canaan was because he was living in the place that we call Iraq today. But, one day, God said to him in essence, I want you to leave everything that you own as well as your family behind and follow me on a journey into the land of Canaan. When you get there, I will let you know where to settle. We see this in **Genesis 12:1-4:**

> **"Now the LORD had said unto Abram, Get thee out of thy country, and from thy kindred, and from thy father's house, unto a land that I will shew thee**: 2 And I will make of thee a great nation, and I will bless thee, and make thy name great; and thou shalt be a blessing: 3 And I will bless them that bless thee, and curse him that curseth thee: and in thee shall all families of the earth be blessed. 4 **So Abram departed, as the LORD had spoken unto him; and Lot went with him: and Abram was seventy and five years old when he departed out of Haran."**

He was seventy-five years old and by the time God finished with him and Isaac was born, he was a 100 years old. **Can you imagine God telling you to follow Him into a strange wilderness land and you wait 25 years for Him to fulfill His promise to you?** This is one of the ultimate tests of faith and this is the God that we are dealing with.

There are aspects of Him that you must know to help you as you journey with Him so that you do not get discouraged in your Christian walk. As we saw in the previous chapter, one thing that He has plenty of is patience or longsuffering. If you are going to be stubborn and rebellious for thirty years, He will sit down and just watch you. He will do nothing until you decide to line up with His purpose; He is God.

## Trust and Obey

The best thing to tell yourself is, trust and obey Him because when He tells you to do something He is not going to change His mind about you doing that thing if it is a condition that He has for you to fulfill before He can move on your behalf. Remember that He said the following in **Isaiah 55:11** about His Word:

> "So shall my word be that goeth forth out of my mouth: it shall not return unto me void, but it shall accomplish that which I please, and it shall prosper in the thing whereto I sent it."

His Word is forever settled in heaven and He does not change it for anyone. Therefore, if anything is going to change, it is going to be you and me. Also, God Himself does not change but He might change His heart and have mercy on us but He does not change His righteous requirements for anyone.

## Sin Brings Shame and Reproach

As I mentioned before, sometimes some people think that God is going to cut them some slack and overlook their indiscretions and their secret sins because they walk so closely with Him. The reason they do this is because they forget about this drastic side of God's demand for righteousness and holiness. In His mercy, God will keep telling them to mend their ways and if they do not listen, then He brings a judgment against them or He allows the devil to make a public spectacle of them. According to the Bible sin brings reproach:

> "Righteousness exalteth a nation: **but sin is a reproach to any people**" (Proverbs 14:34).

This is one of the reasons why the Lord Jesus had to carry His Cross bearing our shame and our sin as He took a humiliating walk to Golgotha. They put Him to shame by making Him to drag His Cross while the soldiers mocked, whipped, and jeered at Him. Some even spat on Him but He went to the Cross bearing all our shame upon Himself. We must never forget that one of the effects of sin is shame. God will allow anyone who refuses to mend their ways or change from their wicked ways to be publicly put to shame even if the person is the biggest and most popular Christian minister.

If you revisit the incident of Adam and Eve in the Garden of Eden, you can see that shame was the first thing Adam and Eve experienced when they heard the voice of the Lord coming to them after they sinned as recorded in **Genesis 3:7-11**:

> "**And the eyes of them both were opened, and they knew that they were naked; and they sewed fig leaves together, and made themselves aprons.** *8* And they heard the voice of the LORD God walking in the garden in the cool of the day: and Adam and his wife hid themselves from the presence of the LORD God amongst the trees of the garden.
>
> *9* And the LORD God called unto Adam, and said unto him, Where art thou? *10* **And he said, I heard thy voice in the garden, and I was afraid, because I was naked; and I hid myself.** *11* And he said, Who told thee that thou wast naked? **Hast thou eaten of the tree, whereof I commanded thee that thou shouldest not eat?** *(this is the sin that brought the shame of nakedness)*."

**Sin leaves you without defense and you become vulnerable to every demon out there that wants to take advantage of you.** Adam and Eve lost their divine defense in God because of their sin and so they felt naked without any divine protection. The devil knew it and he immediately implemented his evil plan to destroy them and their children. As a result, he inspired Cain to kill Abel.

Therefore, the only way that we can walk under God's protective arms and wings is to truly know and live by the Word of God and to get a good understanding of what it means for Him to be God in our lives and on earth so that we can avoid sin.

## God is Not Operating a Democracy

We must all know that **God is not operating a Democratic system of government** *which is a government of the people by the people and for the people.* **Rather, He is operating a Kingdom through His Son Jesus Christ using His church (believers).** As a result, God makes a sovereign decree or decision and humanity's duty as His subjects is to obey Him. His is not a system of government where He has to be politically correct or politically careful not to offend those who are opposed to His kingdom rule and dominion.

In a kingdom, everyone does not get to put their two cents in so that no one is offended or left out. Instead, we are all to know His Word and to obey it without any exception. We cannot add to it or change it and it is not meant to appeal to our flesh or to be compromised to fit our selfish desires and lusts. It is the Word of the Sovereign God and failure to know it, to obey it and to live by it means eternal damnation in hell.

# *Chapter 8*
# God's Blank Check to Every Human Being

## You Decide How Much of God You Want in Your Life

We all get to decide how much of God we want in our lives and how much of Him we want to know. However, how you position yourself to know Him is how He is going to operate and release things to you. There are people that will fast 20 or 40 days and they constantly declare how much they love God but when God commands or gives them instructions, they do not obey. To God, their love is just words with no follow through and fasting is not for God but to help us discipline our flesh.

When we come into God's kingdom as newly born again Christians, we are all taught the same lesson that the children of Israel had to learn. God does not let us go on the rosy path in which everything that our "little hearts" desire magically manifests at our command while we continue to live as hell without any ounce of godly character in us. Instead as I said before, He takes us on a ride that He knows is going to dust off those things that have been cluttering our communication with Him and making us to think too highly of ourselves.

He knows exactly the things that will help Him to remove all that we have been holding up in our lives as gods and the people that we have been idolizing or have been idolizing us. In His attempt to be the only God in our lives and to have the preeminence, He goes after these things to root them out and to cleanse all the foolishness out of us for our own good. The bottom line is that He wants us to make room for Him in our lives and to give Him the preeminence in our lives and in all that we do.

God's blank check to all humanity also includes His love. We all get to decide for ourselves how much of His love we want and how much of our love we want to give Him or have room for in our lives.

## The Test of How Much You Love God

I will say to you up front that you do not love God anymore than you obey His Word. Crying or being emotional when the name of the Lord is spoken does not measure how much you love God. Having goose pumps while jumping and shouting does not measure how much you love God. The Lord Jesus gave us the criteria for measuring how much we love God in **John 14:21-24**:

> **"He that hath my commandments, and keepeth them, he it is that loveth me**: and he that loveth me shall be loved of my Father, and I will love him, and will manifest myself to him. 22 Judas saith unto him, not Iscariot, Lord, how is it that thou wilt manifest thyself unto us, and not unto the world? 23 Jesus answered and said unto him, **If a man love me, he will keep my words: and my Father will love him, and we will come unto him, and make our abode with him.** 24 **He that loveth me not keepeth not my sayings: and the word which ye hear is not mine, but the Father's which sent me."**

Again as you can see from the above scripture, the Lord Jesus gave us **obedience to the Word of God** as the clear litmus test of our love for Him, for the Father and for the Holy Spirit. **I say to you therefore that you love God to the extent that you obey God's Word.** In other words, the extent to which you obey God's Word is the extent that you love Him and it is the extent to which He will operate in your life. Some people obey Him faster and sooner so they love Him more and they see more of His manifestations in their lives.

Other people never act quickly or act at all when they hear from the Lord. They are like stubborn mules that will not respond to commands. They tend to debate within themselves whether or not to obey and in so doing make the Word of God that came to them of none effect. Some of them take counsel from their friends and different other people until they suffer what the Lord calls, "paralysis of analysis."

While they are busy over analyzing rather than obeying God's Word, God finds a "David" somewhere and a David is one that is quick to do the will of the Lord. Some of these people go to church and they sing, they cry and they spread their hands wider than any other person around them but when the Lord looks at them, He sees them as nothing but mules that will not move at His instructions. The Lord will say about them, "See this ones, they do not obey me; they are all show without any substance or godly character. They confirm the word of God in **Matthew 15:8** that says:

> **"This people draweth nigh unto me with their mouth, and honoureth me with their lips; but their heart is far from me."**

We have to know that we are dealing with an awesome God and we also have to understand that there are so many aspects of Him that we need to acquaint ourselves with if we want to walk successfully with Him in our Christian life. He is more than willing to keep us in the straight and narrow path and to deliver us from the broad way that leads to destruction.

Therefore, knowing God's names and knowing what His names reveal about who He is, will help us to avoid the delusions that lead many to believe that they are His favorite children and as such, He will cut them some slack as they continue in sin. People who allow themselves to be so deceived can be walking on the broad way created for them by the devil and not even be aware of it.

## Moses' Benefits of Knowing God's Names

Moses knew how to cash in on God's blank check because he realized the benefits of knowing God's names. He is the author of **Psalms 90 and 91** and when you read them, you will be amazed at the great benefits that he received and that also awaits all those who take the time to know God by His names. Look at what God gave to Moses to write about it in **Psalm 91:14-16:**

> "Because he hath set his love upon me, therefore will I deliver him: **I will set him on high, because he hath known my name.** *15* **He shall call upon me, and I will answer him:** I will be with him in trouble; I will deliver him, and honour him. *16* With long life will I satisfy him, and shew him my salvation."

He said because "**he** (Moses or any other person) **hath known my name, I will set him on high."** Therefore, if you take the time to know the names of God, He has certain blessings for anyone that comes to this level in their walk with Him. Many people read **Psalm 91:14-16** and think that the blessings apply to them but if you do not take the time to study and know His names, you cannot claim these blessings. You must get a personal revelation of what God's names mean to you.

**You must know the significance of the names of God because this was how Moses learned and knew the ways of God!** God has many names and many of them are functional names. For example, you should know Him as your I AM, you should know Him as your Provider; you should know Him as the Self-Existing One and you should know Him by all that His other names reveal about Him.

When you know Him as such, then you will understand what He meant when He declared through Moses in **Psalms 91:15** that, **"He shall call upon me and I will answer Him."**

God answered Moses every time that Moses called upon Him and whenever Moses interceded and pleaded with Him not to do something or bring about His judgment, He listened to Moses.

We too can begin to experience how quickly He answers those who truly know Him by His names. He is the same yesterday, today and forever. What He did for Moses back then, He will do for every one of us and even more if only we will take the time to know Him.

# Conclusion

God wants us to know that He is love, that He forgives, that He is merciful, that He is gracious and that He is also a consuming fire. We are to also know that He knows all things, He sees all things, He owns all things and that He is jealous over man. Yes, He is a jealous God! We must also know Him as our Father, our teacher and our purifier or refiner. There are so many aspects of God that we have to take the time to assimilate.

For instance, just knowing that God is longsuffering alone will make you to be quick to obey Him because if it is going to take you fifty years to obey Him, He is willing to wait that long for you. If you die without obeying Him, He then will wait for your children to grow up to obey Him. This can go on for several generations. Therefore, take the time to know what His names reveal about Him.

God's names are to help us understand Him, to fear Him, to depend on Him and to live by His every Word. As a result, God must bring every single one of us to our knees so that we will know Him and surrender to Him as the Lord our God; the only God in our lives and nothing else. Anything that rivals Him in our lives He will go after until it has a lesser priority in our lives. It does not matter what it is; whether it is your child, your job, your relationships, etc. He will go after it until you know that He alone must have the preeminence in your life as God.

After studying God's names, **I came to the conclusion that God meant for all of His names to help me to love Him, to trust Him, to walk in the fear of Him, to humble me and to help me become obedient to every Word that comes out of His mouth. I am to know that He is God and there is none else besides Him and you are to do the same in your life because God is no respecter of person.** What He requires from one, He also requires from another.

**Your eternity is at stake here.** According to the Lord in **Matthew 5:45,** God is gracious to every human being and allows His sun to shine on the good as well as the evil; He sends His rain on the just as well as the unjust but that does not mean that all will escape His wrath on Judgment Day. Therefore, get to know Him by His name.

**Always remember that besides the Torah and the Bible, no other religion claims to have the actual Word of God and therefore, no other religion can teach you the true knowledge of who God is.** For example, according to Mohammed, the writings in the Islamic Koran were "given" to him by an angel. Those who are Buddhists live by the word of Buddha while others follow the teachings of people like Krishna, Confucius, Zoroaster, etc. **The Jewish Torah and the Christian Bible are the only books that contain the actual Word of God and God Himself testifies to it.** Think about it and may God bless you as you seek to know Him deeper.

—**Dr. Mary J. Ogenaarekhua**

# About the Author

I am a born again Christian who believes in the preservation of human life and the sanctity of marriage as defined by the Bible. Below is the biographical information about me.

## Biographical Information

**Name:** Prophetess Mary J. Ogenaarekhua, PhD (pronounced **Oge-nah-re-qua**).

**Founder**: Mary J. Ministries, Inc.

**Educational Background**: BA Communications-Journalism, Masters Degree in Public Administration and a PhD in Theology

Dr. Mary Justina Ogenaarekhua (a-k-a Mary O.) was born in Nigeria. She grew up in a Muslim home and attended Roman Catholic elementary and high schools. The Lord miraculously raised Mary up from the dead when she took a fatal fall in her early years. Prophetess Mary is gifted with the ability to interpret visions and dreams, to hear the voice of the Lord, to discern spirits and to intercede as a prayer warrior. She is also the Lord's scribe.

Dr. Mary operates in the gift of prophecy with the ability to see into the spiritual realm. God has opened Prophetess Mary's spiritual eyes to see His desire for His people. She's a teacher of the unadulterated Word of God; a true woman of God in rare spiritual form! She holds workshops and conferences as well as teaches and preaches on many topics including **deliverance, healing, visions and dreams, spiritual discernment, understanding the power of covenants,**

**effective prayer, mentoring, leadership training and much more**. She conducts **evangelism and outdoor crusades internationally** with thousands in attendance.

**Dr. Mary Justina Ogenaarekhua is the author of the following books:**

(1) **Unveiling the God-Mother.** This book is a biography of *Mary's death and resurrection experience* and her early years in Africa. It details the spiritual events that happened to her before she became a Christian and before she came to the United States. She also discusses some of the holidays that a lot of Christians celebrate ignorantly.

(2) **Keys to Understanding Your Visions and Dreams: A Classroom Approach.** Prophetess Mary has an eagle's eye that sees far into the realm of the spirit. She was raised from the dead to instruct the body of Christ on how to walk in the realm of the spirit. In this book about visions and dreams, she uses the Word of God to instruct the body of Christ on visions and dreams. She applies the first hand revelation knowledge that she learned from the Lord Himself. This book is a must read for everyone who dreams and everyone who sees visions.

(3) **A Teacher's Manual on Visions and Dreams.** This manual is designed to teach the average person, bishops, pastors, etc., the basic principles about visions and dreams, about sources of vision and dreams, about how to identify the sources of visions and dreams and how to analyze the contents of visions and dreams. It is meant to be used along with the above textbook titled, **Keys to Understanding Your Visions and Dreams**.

(4) **How to Discern and Expel Evil Spirits.** This is a very powerful book for all those who are called to

the healing and deliverance ministry. In it, Dr. Mary answers the questions most people have concerning evil spirits, and she teaches on the origin of evil spirits, how to discern and expel them and she answers the question, "Can a Christian have a demon?" This is a foundational resource for all those who want to walk in great spiritual discernment.

(5) **A Teacher's Manual on Discerning and Expelling Evil Spirits.** This is a powerful teaching guide for those who are called to the healing and deliverance ministry. It is a teacher's tool with a step by step teaching on key principles about evil spirits, the origin of evil spirits and how to identify and expel evil spirits. It is meant to be used along with the above textbook on **How to Discern and Expel Evil Spirits**.

(6) **How I Heard from God: The Power of Personal Prophesy.** Prophetess Mary Ogenaarekhua outlines key principles concerning personal prophecy and she lays out a blue print of what to do with your personal prophetic words. She helps the reader understand the conditions that are attached by God to every personal prophetic word. Failure to understand these conditions will keep your God-given prophetic word from coming to pass.

(7) **Effective Prayers for Various Situations: Volumes I and II.** In *Effective Prayers*, Prophetess Mary outlines and gives principles on how to pray effectively concerning various life situations. It contains prayers for almost every situation that a lot of Christians battle with. Many have given testimonies about the deliverance and blessings manifested in their lives as a result of praying these prayers.

(8) **Keys to Successful Mentoring Relationships.** In this book, Dr. Mary outlines the dynamics involved

in a mentoring relationship and the actual steps and stages of mentoring. She also highlights the pitfalls to avoid.

(9) **A Workbook for Successful Mentoring.** This workbook is a powerful teaching guide for all those who want to be mentored and those who desire to mentor others. It is a teacher/student's valuable tool for teaching and practicing mentoring. It is meant to be used along with the above textbook titled, **Keys to Successful Mentoring Relationships**.

(10) **Understanding the Power of Covenants.** This book teaches on the power of covenants. Covenants impact our lives for good or for bad on a daily basis. It allows us to learn about how God uses covenants, how the devil uses covenants and how God wants us to use covenants so that we can receive what He has for us and avoid the devil's attempts to use negative covenants to hinder us. Negative covenants can hinder a person's progress throughout the person's life.

(11) **Secrets About Writing and Publishing Your Book: What Other Publishers Will Not Tell You.** This book is a powerful synopsis of what you need to know in order to write and get your book published and also how to position your book for mass marketing. It is designed to help all those who desire to write and market their books.

(12) **The Agenda of the Few**. This book is a call for the Church to get back to its God-given purpose for this country which is to reach all Americans for God. For too long now, the Church has been functioning as though it is only called to one political party –the Republican Party. The issues discussed in this book are meant to remind the reader that there are Ten Commandments in the Bible and that God can

choose to address any of these commandments at any given time. Therefore, we must be willing to get the Church out of the Republican Party box that we have placed it in and learn to seek God's will during each presidential election. He is God of both the Republican and Democratic Parties.

(13) **The Agenda of the Masses.** Just like the **"Agenda of the Few"** that was written to the Christian Conservatives in the Republican Party, this book addresses what the Lord showed me that a lot of the Christians in the Democratic Party are doing that equally displeases Him. They have allowed a very large segment of the Church to be pulled away by "the agenda of the masses." In other words, they have bought into the ungodly doctrines, ideologies, beliefs, and political views of the masses to the point that now, their version of Christianity within the Democratic Party is essentially "anything goes."

(14) **What Tribe of Israel Am I From?** This book is designed to answer the questions of some Christians who are trying to determine the tribe of the natural Israel that they are from. The reason they want to know this is because there are some teachings going on in Christendom in which Christians are being assigned to the various tribes of Israel. This book will help anyone to determine the tribe of Israel that they are from. It is an eye opener for anyone who desires to know the truth.

**Dr. Mary O.** lives in Atlanta and is the founder of **Mary J. Ministries** and **To His Glory Publishing Company, Inc.** She is an ordained minister with a strong Deliverance Anointing. She has appeared on Trinity Broadcasting Network and other national television programs.

# About Mary J. Ministries

**Mary J. Ministries** was founded by Dr. Mary J. Ogenaarekhua to equip and impart the Anointing of God to the Body of Christ for the purpose of impacting the whole world. Our mission is to help men, women; old and the young to build relationships through Bible Studies, Community Outreach, Prayer Support, Caring Ministries, Teaching on Visions and Dreams, Discernment/Deliverance, Evangelism, Mentoring, Fellowship and Special Events.

As an ordained minister, Prophetess Mary O. teaches, trains and activates individuals to properly operate their prophetic gifts of discernment, deliverance ministry, outreach ministry (evangelism) and interpretation of visions and dreams. Teachings provided by Prophetess Mary O. are inspired by God and are balanced biblical principles for the purpose of developing a spirit of excellence, wholeness and GODLY character.

Prophetess Mary O. is committed to helping the Body of Christ and those who do not yet know the Lord Jesus as their personal Savior to understand their God-given purpose. Mary J. Ministries regularly hosts classes, seminars, conferences and crusades in the US, Canada as well as other countries.

**Contact Mary J. Ministries:**
Phone: **770-458-7947**
Website: www.maryjministries.org

# About To His Glory Publishing Co.

**To His Glory Publishing Company, Inc.** was also founded by Dr. Mary J. Ogenaarekhua to help writers become published authors. Our goal is to help new and established writers edit, publish and market their work for a reasonable cost.

To His Glory Publishing Company, Inc. offers one of the most cost efficient and stress- free ways of getting a manuscript published.

We also pay one of the highest royalties in the publishing industry –40%!

**Our Services Include:**
- Editing
- Book layout
- Book cover design
- Book manufacturing
- Book distribution (this is a separate and optional service)
- Book placement on Amazon.com, Barnesandnoble.com, Kindle, iPad, and other book marketing sites and devices (these are separate and optional services).

**Contact To His Glory Publishing Company:**
Phone: **770-458-7947**
Website: www.tohisglorypublishing.com

# Bibliography

Josephus, Flavius. *Antiquities of the Jews*, Book 1, Chapter 4:2-3, ( c. 94 AD/CE).

Ogenaarekhua, Mary J. *How to Discern and Expel Evil Spirits*. To His Glory Publishing Company, Lilburn, GA, USA.

Ogenaarekhua, Mary J. Sermon: *How to Move God's Heart*.

# TO HIS GLORY PUBLISHING COMPANY, INC.

## 463 Dogwood Dr. Lilburn, GA. 30047, U.S.A (770)458-7947

## Order Form for Bookstores in the USA

Order Date: _____

Order Placed By: _____     By Fax: _____

Address: _____

_____

City _____ST/ZIP _____

Phone #: _____

Email: _____

Purchase Order#: _____

**Return Policy:** Within 1 year but not before 90 Days.

| **Price** | **Quantity** | **List Price** |
|---|---|---|
|  |  |  |
|  |  |  |
|  |  |  |
|  |  |  |
|  |  |  |
|  |  |  |
|  |  |  |
|  |  |  |
| **Shipping Method:** |  |  |
| **Media:** |  |  |
| **UPS:** |  |  |
| **FedEx:** |  |  |
| **Other (Please Secify):** |  |  |
| **Total Price:** | **Total Quantity:** | **List Price** |

**Ship To Address:**           **Bill to Address:**

# Other Books by Prophetess Mary Ogenaarekhua

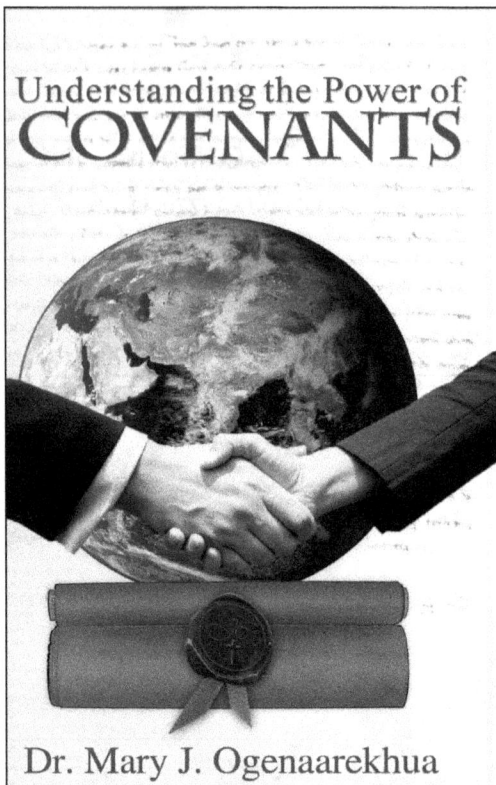

Understanding the Power of
**COVENANTS**

Dr. Mary J. Ogenaarekhua

ISBN 978-0-9791566-8-7

ISBN 978-0-9821900-2-9

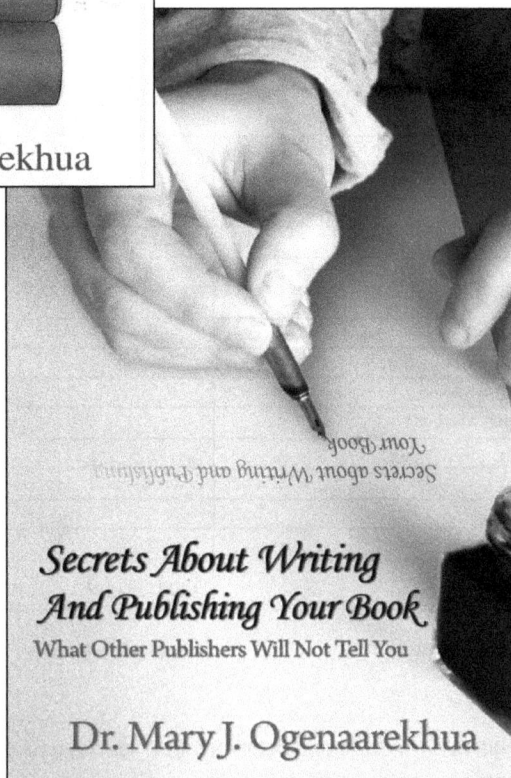

*Secrets About Writing
And Publishing Your Book*
What Other Publishers Will Not Tell You

Dr. Mary J. Ogenaarekhua

Other Books by Prophetess Mary Ogenaarekhua

ISBN 978-0-9774265-6-0

EFFECTIVE PRAYERS
FOR VARIOUS SITUATIONS

Prophetess
Mary J. Ogenaarekhua
AUTHOR OF UNVEILING THE GOD-MOTHER

Vol. 1

ISBN 978-0-9774265-9-1

VE PRAYERS
US SITUATIONS
Vol. II

Prophetess
Mary J. Ogenaarekhua
AUTHOR OF UNVEILING THE GOD-MOTHER

# Other Books by Prophetess Mary Ogenaarekhua

KEYS TO UNDERSTANDING YOUR

VISIONS AND DREAMS

A CLASSROOM APPROACH

MARY J. OGENAAR

AUTHOR OF UNVEILING

ISBN 978-0-9749802-1-8

HOW TO DISCERN AND EXPEL

EVIL SPIRITS

PROPHETESS MARY J. OGENAAREKHUA

AUTHOR OF UNVEILING THE GOD-MOTHER

ISBN 978-0-9749802-8-7

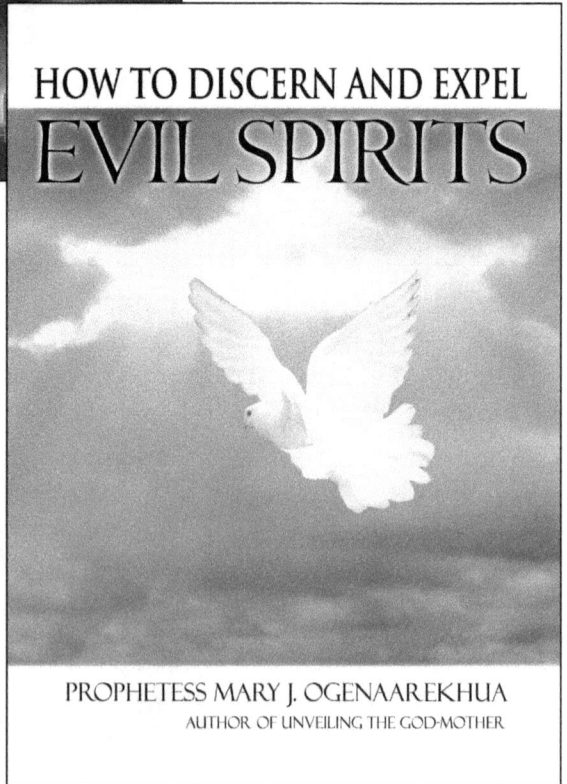

# Other Books by Prophetess Mary Ogenaarekhua

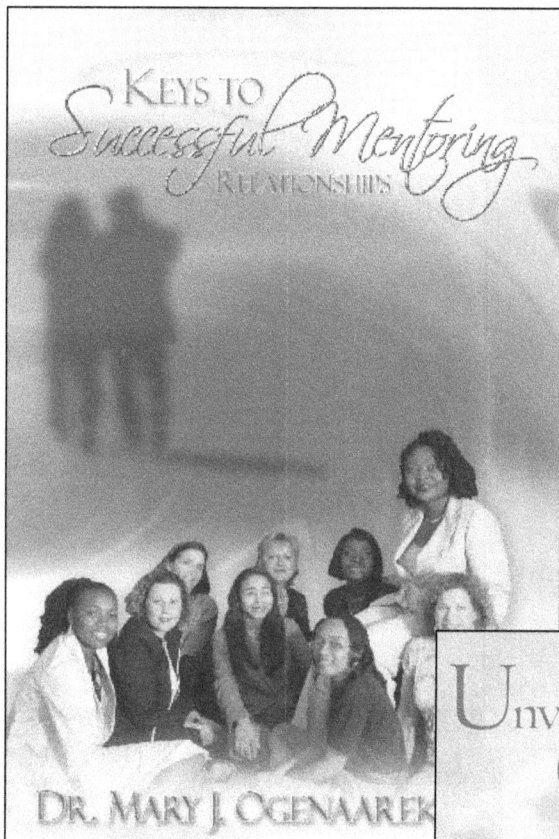

KEYS TO *Successful Mentoring* RELATIONSHIPS

DR. MARY J. OGENAAREK

ISBN 978-0-9791566-6-3

ISBN 978-1-5873628-0-4

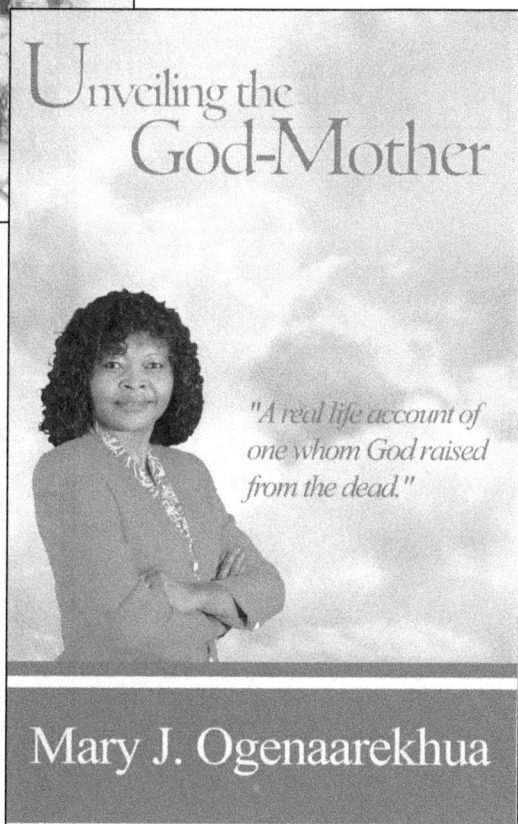

Unveiling the
God-Mother

*"A real life account of one whom God raised from the dead."*

Mary J. Ogenaarekhua

Other Books by Prophetess Mary Ogenaarekhua

ISBN 978-0-9821900-1-2

ISBN 978-0-9821900-4-3

# What Tribe of Israel

Am I From?

Dr. Mary J. Ogenaarekhua

ISBN 978-1-5873628-0-4